Psychical Miscellanea
Being Papers on
Psychical Research, Telepathy,
Hypnotism, Christian Science,
etc.

BY
J. ARTHUR HILL

PREFACE

Many friends and correspondents have suggested that I should republish a number of articles which have appeared from time to time in various quarters. The present volume brings these articles together, with some which have not appeared before.

Each chapter is complete in itself, but there is more or less connexion, for each deals with some aspect of the subject to which I have given most attention during the last twelve years—namely, psychical research.

I thank the editors of the *Holborn Review*, *National Review*, *World's Work*, and *Occult Review* for permission to republish articles which have appeared in their pages.

J. A. H.
Thornton,
Bradford.

CONTENTS

Psychical Miscellanea

DEATH

Our feelings with regard to the termination of our earthly existence are remarkably varied. In some people, there is an absolutely genuine and strong desire for cessation of individual consciousness, as in the case of John Addington Symonds. Probably, however, this is met with only in keenly sensitive natures which have suffered greatly in this life. Such unfortunate people are sometimes constitutionally unable to believe in anything better than cessation of their pain. Anything better than that is "too good to be true", so much too good that they hardly dare wish for it. Others, who have had a happy life, naturally desire a continuance of it, and are therefore eager, like F. W. H. Myers, for that which Symonds dreaded. Others, again, and these are probably the majority, have no very marked feeling in the matter; like the good Churchman in the story, they hope to enter into everlasting bliss, but they wish you would not talk about such depressing subjects. This seems to suggest that they have secret qualms about the reality of the bliss. Perhaps they have read Mark Twain's *Captain Stormfield's Visit to Heaven*, and, though inexpressibly shocked by that exuberant work, are nevertheless tinged with a sneaking sympathy for its hero, who found the orthodox abode of the blest an unbearably dull place. The harp-playing in particular was trying, and he had difficulty in managing his wings.

Anyhow, these people avoid the subject. As Emerson says somewhere, religion has dealings with them three times in their lives: when they are christened, when they are married, and when they are buried. And undoubtedly its main appeal is in the period prior to this third formality, if they happen to have a longish illness. The rich Miss Crawley, in *Vanity Fair,* is typical of many. In days of health and good spirits, this venerable lady had "as free

6

notions of religion and morals as Monsieur de Voltaire himself could desire"; but when she was in the clutches of disease, and even though in the odour of sanctity, so to speak—for she was nursed by Mrs Reverend Bute Crawley, who hoped for the seventy thousand pounds if she could keep Rawdon and Becky off the doorstep—even with this spiritual advantage she was in much fear, and "an utter cowardice took possession of the prostrate old sinner."

Well, let those laugh who will. As for me, I have great sympathy with Miss Crawley. Probably those who laugh, or are contemptuous of such cowardice, are people who have not yet come to close quarters with death—have not looked him, as the French say, in the white of the eyes. Let them wait until that happens. If they come back after that rencontre, they will be a little more tolerant of the cowardice of those whom they called weaker brethren.

Fear of death may be divided into classes, according to its cause, i.e., the intellectual state out of which it seems to arise. It may be due to the expectation of physical suffering; or, as in such cases as Cowper's and Dr Johnson's, to expectation of what may happen after death, in that undiscovered country from which Hamlet said no traveller returned, though he had just been talking with his father's ghost, piping hot—as Goldsmith has it in his Essay on Metaphor—from Purgatory. In my own case, I think the fear is a little of both. And I admit that in both directions the fear is irrational. As to the physical part, it is probable that when my time comes I shall depart without much of what is usually called pain, for the heart seems to be my weak place, and I may reasonably hope that even though if attacked by other ailments, it will be the heart that will give way. There will probably be suffering through difficulty of breathing, and I dread this somewhat, for I know how unpleasant it has been in the attacks which I have survived. Still, it can hardly be compared with the agonising pain of many diseases. Rationally, then, I ought not to have much fear on the physical side.

On the spiritual side I confess with Oliver Wendell Holmes that I have never quite got from under the shadow of the orthodox hell. I had a Puritan upbringing, not severe in its home theology I am thankful to say, but involving attendance at an Independent Chapel where the minister—a good man and no hypocrite—was wont to preach very terrible sermons. I shall never quite get over the baneful effect of those damnatory fulminations. They branded my soul. They caused me more pain than anything else has ever done throughout my life—and this is saying a great deal. They made me hate God. Remember, I was a defenceless child. I knew of no other God. I thought all decent people believed like those about me. I was the only heretic—a rebel, an outlaw, an Ishmael. Conceive, if you can, the agony of a sensitive child struggling with that thought! Condemned to eternal torment, with those who, in Dante's terrible line, "have no hope of death." ("Inferno," iii, 46.)

Then I fell in with O. W. Holmes's Autocrat and Professor, and found a friendly hand in the darkness. It led me to Emerson and Carlyle; then I found Darwin, Spencer, and the rest of them. My loneliness was mitigated, but the seared place in my soul was not healed, and never will be healed. I cannot read the Inferno and Purgatorio of Dante without horror, and thus the poetic beauty of those great cantos is darkened for me. I cannot worship "God," for "God" is the fiend whose image was stamped into my mind in its most plastic, most defenceless period. Truly that early teaching has much to answer for. It has poisoned a great part of my life. I suppose if I could have "accepted" that Being as my God, accepting also the sacrifice—the Blood—by which that Being's anger was supposed to be assuaged—I suppose I should have been happy, feeling myself "saved." (But I have lately been surprised to find how ineffective this belief can be. An acquaintance of mine, an orthodox churchwoman who has no religious doubts, and who talks much of the Bible, confesses to "a fear of death which clouds even her brightest moments"—an ever-present, unconquerable dread.) However, I could not accept the dogma. Why, I don't know. Somehow my whole mind and heart revolted against the entire plan of salvation. I never believed any of it. I felt it could not be true. And yet it tortured me. Illogical? Yes: human beings are illogical. I am no exception. The Christian who believes he will go to heaven is equally illogical in his unwillingness to die.

When or if we succeed in getting rid of hell, the spiritual fear of death becomes less torturing, remaining only as a vague dread, as in Hamlet's soliloquy. Bacon says that we fear death as children fear to go in the dark. In my own case, it is somewhat thus that the fear now presents itself. The old hell-fear, though not utterly obliterated, is becoming less all-swallowing. This very desirable state of affairs is partly the result of the conclusions to which I have been led by psychical research. After many years of experiment and close study, I can say that I know something about after-death conditions. Not that I pretend to be able to coerce other people into a similar belief, even if I wanted to. Each must travel his own path. Moreover, psychical research being a science, its results are not more certain than those of other sciences. Alternative theories in explanation of any phenomenon are always possible. There is no such thing as knock-down proof. But for my part I can say that I know—in the same way that I know the truth of Mendeleef's law, or Avogadro's law, or Dalton's atomic theory—that human beings do not become extinct when they die, that they are often able to communicate with us after that event, and that they are not in any orthodox heaven or hell. My knowledge is based partly on a lengthy and carefully-conducted series of sittings which some intimate friends of mine have had with a medium known to me; partly on my own results over a period of several years of systematic investigation; and partly on various curious experiences of psychic friends of mine who are in no sense professional mediums. (Details to some extent in my *New Evidences in Psychical Research* (Rider, 1911) and *Psychical Investigations* (Cassell, 1917.) I now believe, with the Bishop of London, that a man is essentially the same five minutes after death as he was five minutes before. As the old woman says in *David Copperfield*, "death doesn't change us more than life"—no, nor as much!

The upshot is, of course, that my spiritual fear of death has, I am thankful to say, almost vanished. The lurid future has taken on a milder radiance.

It is not that I want assuring of "happiness" in a future state as compensation for misery in this. I should be quite contented if I could be assured that death is annihilation. It would at least be a cessation of suffering; and that is much. I could agree with Keats:

"Darkling I listen; and, for many a time I have been half in love with easeful Death, Called him soft names in many a muséd rhyme, To take into the air my quiet breath. Now more than ever seems it rich to die, To cease upon the midnight with no pain While thou art pouring forth thy soul abroad In such an ecstasy. Still wouldst thou sing, and I have ears in vain— To thy high requiem become a sod!" —(*To the Nightingale*)

Easeful death—it is a good word. Keats knew disease, and was content with prospect of ease; though at the end there is a note of depression or despair at the thought of becoming a "sod," deaf and blind to beauty.

This reminds us of the attitude of other poets towards the great problem. Tennyson is mildly optimistic and placid; stretches, indeed, somewhat lame hands of faith in his sorrowful moments when his friend has died, but on the whole is healthily disposed; friendly to the most cheerful way of looking at it; inclined, with true British burliness, to make the best of a bad job—a job which, after all, may not be so very bad when we come to closer quarters with it. Afar, death is the spectre feared of man; seen nearer, he may metamorphose into a beautiful Iris, sent by heavenly mercy. And, afterwards, the new spiritual state will probably be an improvement—Aeonian evolution through all the spheres. Therefore, away with all selfish mourning either about our own prospective fate or that of those who have left us. Let us hate the black negation of the bier:

"And wish the dead, as happier than ourselves And higher, having climb'd one step beyond Our village miseries, might be borne in white To burial or to burning, hymned from hence With songs in praise of death, and crowned with flowers."

No doubt Tennyson was to a very great extent able to stay himself on the personal mystic experiences described in his poem *The Ancient Sage*—experiences which gave him a subjective assurance that death was "a ludicrous impossibility". Browning, characteristically buoyant, was ready to face death with a laugh; the fog in the throat will pass, the black minute's at end, then thy breast. In *Prospice* we feel the eager sureness with which he looked forward to rejoining her whose bodily presence had left him a few months before. But even Browning's cheery salutation is outdone by Whitman. The American, though acquainted with suffering as Browning was not, and though apparently without much belief or interest in personal survival, was almost uncannily friendly to his own taking off. And it was not because he suffered so greatly that he hailed release. It was more the natural outcome of his joyous temperament, subdued at the last to a kind of solemn exaltation. The following stanzas were written with George Inness' picture *The Valley of the Shadow of Death* in mind:

"Nay, do not dream, designer dark, Thou hast portray'd or hit thy theme entire; I, hoverer of late by this dark valley, by its confines, having glimpses of it, Here enter lists with thee, claiming my right to make a symbol too. For I have seen many wounded soldiers die, After dread suffering—have seen their lives

11

pass off with smiles, And I have watch'd the death-hours of the old; and seen the infant die; The rich, with all his nurses and his doctors; And then the poor, in meagreness and poverty; And I myself for long, O Death, have breath'd my every breath Amid the nearness and the silent thought of thee.

"And out of these and thee, I make a scene, a song (not fear of thee, Nor gloom's ravines, nor bleak, nor dark—for I do not fear thee, Nor celebrate the struggle, or contortion, or hard-tied knot), Of the broad blessed light, and perfect air, with meadows, rippling tides, and trees and flowers and grass, And the low hum of living breeze—and in the midst God's beautiful eternal right hand, Thee, holiest minister of Heaven—thee, envoy, usherer, guide at last of all, Rich, florid, loosener of the stricture-knot called life, Sweet, peaceful, welcome Death."

This is indeed a change from the idea of Death as King of Terrors, as "spectre feared of man". (*In Memoriam*)

The Greek idea, at its best, seems to have been half-way between the two extremes. It regarded death with more or less equanimity, as being certainly not the greatest evil—no king of terrors—but merely an emissary of greater Powers, to whose will we must bow, though with dignity:

"He that is a man in good earnest must not be so mean as to whine for life, and grasp intemperately at old age; let him leave this point to Providence."—(Plato: *Gorgias*)

Sophocles has the same thought, with an added touch of Hamlet-like irritation about the slings and arrows of outrageous fortune:

"It is a shame to crave long life, when troubles Allow a man no respite. What delight Bring days, one with another, setting us Forward or backward on our path to death? I would not take the fellow at a gift Who warms himself with unsubstantial hopes; But bravely to live on, or bravely end, Is due to gentle breeding. I have said."—(*Ajax*)

Cicero voices the same pagan feeling, in the contented language of a rather tired, wise old man:

"I look forward to my dissolution as to a secure haven, where I shall at length find a happy repose from the fatigues of a long voyage."—(*De Senectute*)

And was it not Cato—fine old Stoic—who, finding his natural force abating, and accepting the hint furnished by a stumble in the street, stooped and kissed the ground: "Proserpine, I come!" and went home, making a speedy end, unwilling to suffer the indignity of disease and the shame of being served in weakness? Modern opinion wisely reprobates suicide, but there is something noble in the Roman attitude, condemn it as we will. As a modern and almost comic example of a modern Stoic's attitude to this same question of death we may cite the famous lines of Walter Savage Landor:

"I strove with none, for none was worth my strife, Nature I loved, and, next to Nature, Art, I warmed both hands before the fire of life, It sinks, and I am ready to depart."

"Strove with none", indeed! As a matter of fact, Landor strove with everybody. He was one of the most quarrelsome men that ever lived. The only man who could tolerate him was Browning. But in his mellower moments, at least, he was "ready to depart", quietly acquiescing in the scheme of things. To depart, note; not to be extinguished. And this view is, all things considered, the most sane and wholesome view of the great problem of Death. We did not begin to live when we were born in this present tenement of flesh; we shall not cease to live when we quit it. 'Tis but a tent for a night, an interlude, a descent into matter, a temporary incarnation for educative purposes, of the soul or a

13

part of it, as it pursues its lone way towards the ineffable goal. This life is but a sleep and a forgetting;

"The soul that rises with us, our life's star, Has had elsewhere its setting, and cometh from afar."

Death, then, is to be welcomed when it comes. We must not run to meet it, or run from it; but we should welcome it when God thinks fit to send it, His messenger. The beautiful eternal right hand beckons, and the soul gladly arises and departs, to "that imperial palace whence it came", or to fare forth on some "adventure brave and new".

IF A MAN DIE,
SHALL HE LIVE AGAIN?

A friend of mine tells me that psychical articles are always interesting, "because so many people die and go somewhere". Presumably, those who remain here feel a natural curiosity as to where the departed have gone, partly for the latter's sake, and partly because they themselves would like to know, so that they will know what to expect when their own time comes.

The teaching of religion on this point is admittedly either rather vague, or, if definite—as with the Augustinian theology—no longer credible. We have progressed in sensitiveness and humanity, and can no longer believe that a good God will inflict everlasting torment in a lake which burneth with fire and brimstone, even on the most wicked of His creatures. Still less can we believe in such punishment being inflicted for the "sin of unbelief", for we now know well enough that "belief", being the net outcome of our total experience and character, is not under the control of the will. Consequently, a God who punished creatures for not believing, when He knew all the time that He had so constructed most of them that they could not believe, would be either wicked or insane. This inability to believe "to order" is plainly perceived if we reflect on what our feelings would be if a Mohammedan implored us to believe in Allah and in Allah's Prophet, as the only way of salvation. We should decline, saying perhaps that we knew better; but the real reason of our disbelief would not lie in our knowledge but in our general makeup. We could not believe in Mohammedanism if we tried. We have grown up in a different climate, and have taken a different form.

But, putting aside the vindictive hell-god of Augustine, Tertullian, Calvin, and the rest—for not even an earthly father would punish a child for ever—and taking Christianity at its best, we do not find any very specific eschatological teaching. And this very absence is a good feature. If a man tries to be good merely in order to avoid hell and gain heaven—in other words, because it will pay—his goodness is not much of a credit to him. It is only selfishness of a far-sighted kind. Religion, on the other hand, when at its best, seeks to influence character, not by threats and promises, but by encouraging moods and attitudes and habits of thought from which good actions will flow spontaneously, without any profit-and-loss calculations. Modern Christianity is therefore perhaps right in touching much more lightly on the future state than was customary in earlier centuries.

Nevertheless, we cannot repress a little curiosity. People die and go somewhere, as my friend says. Where do they go? Modern Religion having avoided definite answer, we turn to Science. And Science, much as it would surprise such fine old gladiators as Huxley and Tyndall to hear it—has an answer, and an affirmative one.

Psychical research has, in my opinion, brought together a mass of evidence strong enough to justify the following conclusions. I do not say they are "proved." You cannot "prove" that the earth is round, unless your hearer will at least study the evidence. You cannot even prove to him that 2 plus 2 makes 4, if he refuses to add. Therefore I do not say anything about proof. I say only that after many years of careful study and investigation I am of opinion that the evidence justifies the conclusions.

(I) Telepathy is a fact. A mind may become aware of something that is passing in another mind at a distance, by means other than the normal sensory channels. The "how" of the communication is entirely unknown. The analogy of wireless telegraphy of course suggests itself, but is misleading. The ether-waves employed in wireless telegraphy are physical pulses which obey the law of inverse squares; telepathy shows no conformity with that law, and has not been shown to be an affair of physical waves at all. I believe that it is not a physical process; that it occurs in the spiritual world, between mind and mind, not primarily between brain and brain. And, if so—if mind can communicate with mind independently of brain—the theory of materialism at least is exploded. If mind can act independently of brain, mind may go on existing after brain dies.

(2) Communications, purporting to emanate from departed spirits, are sometimes so strikingly evidential that it is scientifically justifiable to assume the agency of a discarnate mind. For example, in a case known to me, a "spirit" communicating through a non-professional medium—a lady of means and position—referred to a recipe for pomatum which the communicator said she had written in her recipe book. No one knew anything about it; but, on hunting up the book, the deceased lady's daughters found a recipe for Dr Somebody's pomade, which their mother had evidently written shortly before her death. They confirmed that "pomatum" was the word which their mother used. The points to be noted are: That the medium was not a professional; that no one who knows her has doubted her integrity; that she was not acquainted with either the deceased lady or her daughters; that the knowledge shown was not possessed by any living (incarnate) mind, and is therefore not explainable by telepathy; and, finally, that the case was watched and reported on by one of our ablest investigators—a lecturer at Newnham College—who found no flaw in the evidence.[1] I repeat that I do not claim this to be "proof". I give it merely as an illustration, and will give a few more detailed cases in a later chapter. For the present I must be content to say that the mass of evidence known to me justifies the belief that minds survive what we call death.

---

[1] *Proceedings of the Society for Psychical Research*, vol. xvii, pp. 181-3.

The question then arises: What is the nature of the after life? And here we are faced with great difficulties. We can ask the returning spirits, but we cannot verify their statements. If my uncle John Smith purports to communicate, I can test his identity by asking him to tell me intimate family details which I can verify by asking his widow, who still lives; but I cannot thus check his statements about his spiritual surroundings. Still, if he has proved his identity—particularly if telepathy seems excluded—we may perhaps feel fairly safe in accepting his other statements as true, or at least in admitting their possible truth. And of course we can obtain the statements of many different spirits, and can compare them. This has been done. The result is a striking amount of uniformity. The various spirits agree, on the main points.

First of all, they are surprisingly unorthodox! They tell of no heaven or hell of the traditional kind. There is no sudden ascent into unalloyed and eternal bliss for the good—who, as Jesus pointed out, are not wholly good—and no sudden plunge into eternal fires for the bad—who, similarly, are not unqualifiedly bad. There is much of bad in the best of us, and much of good in the worst of us. Accordingly, the released soul finds itself not very different from what it was while in the flesh. It has passed into a higher class of the universal school—that is all. Tennyson has the idea exactly:

"No sudden heaven, nor sudden hell, for man, But through the Will of One who knows and rules— And utter knowledge is but utter love— Aeonian Evolution, swift or slow, Thro' all the Spheres—an ever opening height, An ever lessening earth."

I have said that this view is unorthodox, and so it is, if compared with the orthodoxy of Calvin or Edwards or Tertullian. But it is pleasant to find that orthodoxy to-day is a different thing, and that the Tennysonian notion is backed up in high quarters. The Bishopric of London is the highest ecclesiastical office in England, after the Archbishoprics of Canterbury and York, and we find the present Bishop of London (Dr Winnington-Ingram) speaking as follows:

"Is there anything definite about death in the Bible? I believe there is. I think if you follow me, you will find there are six things revealed to us about life after death. The first is that the man is the same man. Instead of death being the end of him, he is exactly the same five minutes after death as five minutes before death, except having gone through one more experience in life. In the second place the character grows after death; there is progress. As it grows in life so it grows after death. A third thing is, we have memory. 'Son, remember', that is what was said to Dives in the other world. Memory for places and people. We shall remember everything after death. And with memory there will be recognition; we shall know one another. Husband and wife, parents and children. Sixthly, we still take great interest in the world we have left".

The good Bishop gets all this out of the Bible, and quite rightly. We hope no heresy-hunter will accuse him of "selecting" his texts and ignoring the hell-fire ones.

So far as earth-language can go, the foregoing represents the probable truth regarding the after life. If we inquire for details, we shall get nothing very satisfactory. If we ask a spirit concerning what he does—how he occupies himself—he will either say he "cannot explain so that you will understand" or will tell about living in houses, going to lectures, teaching children, and the like. All this is obviously symbolical. Any communications that a discarnate entity can send must, to be intelligible to us, be in human earth-language; and this language is based on sense-experience. After death, experience is different, for we no longer have the same bodily senses—eyes, ears, etc.: consequently no explanation of the nature of spiritual existence can be more than approximately true; yet such expressions as living in houses, going to lectures, and the like, may be as near the truth as earth-language can get. If a bird tried to describe air-life to a fish, the best it could do would be to say it is something like water-life, but there is more light, more ease of movement, more detail, more things of interest and beauty. Of the wonders of sound—skylark's song, human choruses, instrumental symphonies—no idea could be conveyed to the fish. Probably our friends in the next stage of existence have, in addition to the experiences which they can partly describe, other experiences of which they can give us absolutely no idea. They have been promoted. Their interests and activities have become wider, their joys greater. Yet they are the "same" souls, as the butterfly is the "same" as the chrysalis from which it has arisen. But to know exactly what it feels like to be a butterfly, the caterpillar and chrysalis have to wait Nature's time. So must we.

PSYCHICAL RESEARCH: ITS METHOD, EVIDENCE, AND TENDENCY.

Spiritualism and Psychical Research are to the fore just now, and there is much newspaper and vocal discussion, based for the most part on ignorance, particularly as regards the violent attackers of these things. It is desirable that exact knowledge of the subject should become more general, and in a recent volume I have tried to review the whole subject impartially.[2]

But there are many who in these stressful days have no time for even one volume on this kind of thing, and for them, or such of them as may read this, I have tried in the present article to give an idea of what psychical research is, on the spiritualistic side, omitting the medical side which concerns itself with suggestive therapeutics. The article was first written as a paper which was read before a society of clergy in Bradford, whose request for it was a significant and pleasing indication that ministers are aware of the importance of the subject. They are realising that psychical research is a powerful support to religious faith, and that its results provide comfort for the bereaved. We live in a scientific age, and the sorrowing heart asks for more than a text and an assurance that it is God's will and all for the best; it asks whether it is a fact that the departed one still lives and knows and loves, whether it is well with him, and whether there will be reunion "over there". Psychical research enables us to answer these questions in the affirmative. Science is now backing up religion, and is providing ministers with by far the best weapon against materialism and so-called rationalism. It meets these negative 'isms on their own ground, and does not need to take cover under intuition or personal religious experience, which are convincing

---

[2] *Spiritualism: Its History, Phenomena, and Doctrine* (Cassell & Co., Ltd.).

21

only to the experient. I am not belittling these; I am only saying that the phenomenal evidence is more potent for the scientific type of mind, and that a knowledge of this evidence is useful to those who are defending religion.

TELEPATHY

It is found by experiment that ideas can be communicated from mind to mind through channels other than the known sensory ones. Professor Gilbert Murray of Oxford, probably the most famous Greek scholar in this country, recently carried out some interesting experiments of this kind in his own family. He would go into another room, leaving his wife and daughter to decide on something which they would try to communicate to him on his return. They chose the most absurd and unlikely things, but in a large number of cases Professor Murray, by making his mind as passive as possible and saying the first thing that came into his head, was able to reproduce with startling accuracy the idea they had in mind. For instance, they thought of Savonarola at Florence and the people burning their clothes and pictures and valuables. Says Professor Murray: "I first felt 'This is Italy', then, 'this is not modern'; and then hesitated, when accidentally a small tarry bit of coal tumbled out of the fire. I smelt oil or paint burning and so got the whole scene. It seems as though here some subconscious impression, struggling up towards consciousness, caught hold of the burning coal as a means of getting through".[3] On another occasion they thought of "Grandfather at the Harrow and Winchester cricket match, dropping hot cigar-ash on Miss Thompson's parasol." Professor Murray's guess, reported verbatim, was: "Why, this is grandfather! He's at a cricket match—why it's absurd: he seems to be dropping ashes on a lady's parasol." Another time they thought of a scene in a book of

---

[3] *Proceedings of the Society for Psychical Research*, vol. 29, p. 59. (For brevity's sake I shall hereinafter use the recognised initials "S.P.R." for the Society.)

Strindberg's which Professor Murray had not read: a poor, old, cross, disappointed schoolmaster eating crabs for lunch at a restaurant, and insisting on having female crabs. Professor Murray says: "I got the atmosphere, the man, the lunch in the restaurant on crabs, and thought I had finished, when my daughter asked: 'What kind of crabs?' I felt rather impatient and said: 'Oh, Lord, I don't know: female crabs.' That is, the response to the question came automatically, with no preparation, while I thought I could not give it. I may add that I had never before heard of there being any inequality between the sexes among crabs, regarded as food."

This kind of evidence is not the best, because the thoughts of members of one family run more or less in similar grooves; though the experimenters recognised this and chose unlikely things purposely. Other investigators have sometimes used cards, drawing one at random from a shuffled pack, looking at it, and the percipient then trying to say what it is. The chance of success is of course one in fifty-two, and the amount of success which we might expect by chance in any series can be mathematically determined. In one series of successful experiments conducted by Sir Oliver Lodge the odds against an explanation by chance alone were about ten millions to one. In ordinary matters this would be regarded as proof.

Other experiments of the same general character have been carried out by Sir William Barrett, Professor Sidgwick, and others, and details may be found in the S.P.R. *Proceedings*. In most cases the idea comes into the mind as an impression, but if the percipient is a good visualiser it is sometimes seen almost externalised as a hallucination. This leads us to the next step.

If it is possible to convey to another mind—sometimes so vividly that the thing is almost seen as if out there in space—an image of scenes thought about, may it not be possible to convey an image of oneself? This idea occurred to a gentleman referred to by Myers as Mr S. H. B. in his book *Human Personality and Its*

Survival of Bodily Death. Mr S. H. B., whom I know by correspondence and whose brother I have known personally for many years, decided that he would try to make himself visible to two young ladies whom he knew, and he concentrated his mind on the effort just before going to bed. He willed to show himself in their room at one o'clock in the morning. The distance from his house to theirs was three miles. Next time he saw them, a few days later, they told him they had had a great fright: the elder sister had seen Mr B.'s apparition, had screamed and awakened her little sister, who also saw him. The time was one o'clock in the morning. They told him this before he said anything about his experiment, and they had no reason to expect that he would try anything of the kind. Both Mr B. and his brother are keen and successful business men; Mr S. H. B. is now retired, his brother is still the head of a large firm. I mention this because some critics seem to have a notion that psychical researchers are a crowd of long-haired poets or semi-lunatic cranks.

PHANTASMS OF THE DEAD

Now if a living man can by force of will project a telepathic phantasm of himself, it is reasonable to suppose that a dead man can do the same, if the so-called dead man still exists; for telepathy does not seem to be a physical process of ether-waves, does not conform to the law of inverse squares or propagate itself in all directions as physical forces do. It seems to occur in the mental world, between mind and mind rather than between brain and brain. Consequently, telepathy from the dead is likely to be easier than from the living, for they over there are not clogged with the fleshly body. Certainly, however they may be explained, there are many cases of the apparition of a deceased person. The difficulty about accepting the evidentiality of some of them is that if the percipient knew that the person appearing was dead, the apparition may be merely a subjective hallucination. And even if the death was not known, it might be surmised, and the apparition might be the result of expectancy if the person appearing was known to be ill or in danger. But there are some cases in which a certain amount of detail is conveyed, rendering a subjective explanation not very probable. For instance, Captain Colt had a vision of his brother, in a kneeling position, with a bullet wound in his right temple. He described the vision to several people in the house before any news came, so the case does not rest on his word alone. In due time information arrived that his brother had been killed. He had been shot through the right temple, had fallen among a heap of others, and was found in a kneeling position. In his pocket was a letter from Capt. Colt asking him, if anything happened to him, to make his presence known in the room in which as a matter of fact the apparition was seen. The vision, it was found, occurred a few hours after the death. Mr Myers gives full details in *Human Personality*. In this case the bullet-wound and the kneeling position are points of correct detail which are hardly explicable on a subjective theory. The best sceptical theory is that the incident was telepathic, the wounded brother sending out his telepathic message after being shot. This is possible, but hardly probable; for death in the case of a bullet-wound through the temple must be almost instantaneous.

Spontaneous cases of this kind and of this degree of evidentiality are rare, but there is a large mass of evidence of the same general character. The S.P.R. once carried out an extensive inquiry, receiving answers from 17,000 people, and tabulating the results in a volume of the *Proceedings*. The final conclusion, expressed in weighed and guarded words, was that "Between deaths and apparitions of the dying person a connexion exists which is not due to chance alone". This was signed, among other members of the Committee, by Professor Sidgwick, whom Professor James once called "the most exasperatingly critical mind in England". Some of the apparitions occur before the person's actual death, but usually in such cases he is already unconscious and the spirit practically free. As to those occurring after, the main difficulty about admitting them as proof of survival is, as just said, the possibility that although they may appear after the death of the person, the telepathic impulse may have been sent out before, and may have remained latent for some time in the mind of the percipient. This has been carefully considered by investigators, and in many cases there are reasons for regarding it as an insufficient theory. On the whole, the evidence tends more and more to suggest that in at least some instances these happenings are due to the agency of a discarnate mind. The proof is cumulative, and no single case can be crucial. There is no coerciveness about it, and each can invent his own hypothesis. But those who have considered the subject most carefully have come to the provisional conclusion that the agency of the so-called dead is in some cases a reasonable, and indeed the most reasonable, supposition. There are of course many narratives of this kind in the Bible,[4] the *Lives* of the Saints, and other literature, but these records, being of pre-scientific date, and lacking the corroborative testimony which we now require, are of a lower order of evidentiality. The new evidence, however, is throwing a backward light on many of these ancient stories, and making them credible once more. To me personally, the Bible is a much more living book than it used to be. I believe that many things in it which I used to regard as myths may have been facts.

NORMAL CLAIRVOYANCE

There are instances, then, of people occasionally having visions which seem to be in some way caused by departed persons. Sometimes the percipient has only one experience of the kind in his life; more often he has several, for this seeing power is somehow temperamental—a sort of gift, like the alleged second sight of the Highlander. It was well known to St Paul, as his reference to "discerning of spirits" shows (I *Cor.*, xii). With some people the experience is fairly common. And in a very few persons the gift is so strong that it is to some extent under

---

[4] *E.g.*, Moses and Elias on the Mount.

control. I say to some extent, and I wish to use words very carefully and to have them understood very clearly at this point. I know several people, who by putting themselves into a passive and receptive condition, but without any trance state, can generally get evidential messages from somewhere; that is, messages embodying facts which the sensitive did not normally know. And some of this matter seems to be due to telepathy from the dead. But it cannot be done at will. I believe that professional mediums who sit for all comers for a fee are often, and indeed generally, quite honest people, but that they cannot distinguish between their own imaginations and what really comes through. Professor Murray, when saying what came into his head, did not know whether it was right or not; that is, he did not know, until he was told, whether he had really got the thing telepathically or whether it was an idea thrown up by his own imagination. So with professional mediums. They give out the ideas that come to them, but as a rule they cannot distinguish; and, the power not being entirely under control, there is often a large mixture of their own imagination.

I have, however, the good fortune to be acquainted with a sensitive who has the unusual power of being able to distinguish; and this is a great advantage, rendering verbatim note-taking much easier, and eliminating any necessity for balancing hits against misses. If nothing comes, he sits silent or talks ordinarily. If he gets anything, it is practically always correct. The amount of his success varies, and he will not sit for people in general. I know many people who have asked him to visit them, offering handsome payment, but he usually declines. He says he cannot do it to order, and would be upset if he failed and caused disappointment. He comes to me, however, because I understand and always tell him that he need not worry if he gets nothing. In fact the meeting is regarded as a social call and not as a séance. We talk for a while about ordinary things, and in half-an-hour or so, if the medium can get his mind placid enough and is in good trim generally, he will begin to see and describe spirits present, often getting their names and all sorts of details. These come for the most part in flashes, and I take down every word he says, in shorthand, without giving any help or indication as to whether he is right or wrong. Sometimes in a whole afternoon he will have only one or two of these gleams, and on one occasion he got nothing. With conditions at their best he will talk almost continuously for an hour, the flashes following each other closely; and sometimes a spirit will remain visible for several minutes, moving about the room. About a dozen of these interviews are described in detail in my book *Psychical Investigations*, and other investigations of the same sensitive by two very able friends of mine in another town are described in *New Evidences in Psychical Research*.

Perhaps one or two illustrative incidents may make things clearer.

The first time Wilkinson came to see me he said, in the middle of ordinary talk, that he saw with me the form of a woman who looked about fifty-four, and whom he described, saying further that her name was Mary. Taking up a piece of paper and a pencil, he wrote in an abstracted manner the words "Roundfield Place". He looked at it, without reading it aloud, then said: "That will be a house", and proceeded to write something else. I got up to look, and found "Roundfield Place. Yes" (the "Yes" written in answer to his remark "That will be a house") and a signature "Mary". Now it happens that my mother's name was Mary, that the description applied to her, and that she died, in 1886, at Roundfield Place, not the house to which Wilkinson came, whither we removed in 1897. Other similar things were said, about other deceased relatives, all true.

In this kind of thing it is our duty to stick to known causes before admitting unknown, and my first supposition was that Wilkinson had primed himself with information. He could have ascertained most of the things by local inquiry, though it would not be very easy, for my mother had been dead twenty-two years,

28

and only middle-aged or elderly people would remember her. Further interviews with him, however, soon carried me beyond the fraud theory—for holding which I now apologise to him, feeling considerably ashamed—for he gave me messages from many people whose association with me I feel sure he did not know, and also some family matter of a very private kind, characteristic of the spirit who purported to be communicating, but known to only four living people. I then fell back on telepathy, assuming that the medium was reading my mind. But, pursuing my investigations, I received information which I did not know but which turned out true. For example, Wilkinson on one occasion described a Ruth and Jacob Robertshaw, giving details about them and saying that Ruth had a very spiritual appearance, with a sort of radiance about her, indicating that she had been a very good woman, and giving other particulars. All this meant nothing to me, for the names were unknown. But, as I had on some other occasions found that spirits were described who were relatives of my last visitor, I asked the person who had last entered the room—except inhabitants of the house—whether she had known people of these names. It turned out that they were connexions of hers with whom she had been in close touch during life, and everything said by the medium was correct. Now in the first place this incident ruled out fraud, for Miss North's visit had occurred three days before, and Wilkinson would have had to have detectives watching both doors of my house, from first thing in the morning to the last thing at night, to find out who my last visitor had been; or he would have had to be in league with a servant or a neighbour, and even thus could hardly have succeeded, for servants are sometimes out—moreover, similar things have happened during the *régime* of different servants—and neighbours could not easily watch both doors during dark winter evenings. Further, our neighbours are friends of ours, non-spiritualists, and not acquainted with Wilkinson. And, after getting to know who my last visitor was, information about her deceased relatives would have had to be hunted up. I could give further reasons for believing that fraud was an untenable hypothesis, but I must be brief. What, next, about telepathy? Well, I had no conscious knowledge of these people, so the medium could not have got his information from my conscious mind. It is possible to assume that I knew it subliminally, and that the medium abstracted it from those hidden levels of my mind. This is a guess, but a legitimate guess. It is the guess that Miss Dougall (author of *Pro Christo et Ecclesia*) makes in criticising this very incident in the book of essays called *Immortality*, by Canon Streeter and others. She suggests that on the occasion of Miss North's visit my mind had photographed the contents of hers, without my knowing it, and that the medium developed the photograph and read off the required information. It may be so, but it seems to me far-fetched. Miss Dougall, I may add, is a member of the S.P.R., and her criticism is instructed criticism, worthy of careful attention. But I cannot accept her theory, which seems to me more wonderful and to require more credulity than the spirit theory. For it is to be observed that the assumed mind-reading is of a character quite different from anything that has been experimentally established. In telepathic experiments, like those of Professor Murray, some incarnate person is *trying* to communicate the thought. This is not the case in my sittings with Wilkinson. I am not trying to communicate anything to him; very much the contrary. And I do not find, after long and careful observation, any parallelism between what he says and what I happen to be thinking about. There is, in short, no evidence for the supposition that my mind is read. The evidence points unmistakably to discarnate agency—telepathy *from the dead*.

TRANCE

The sort of thing I have described is usually known as normal clairvoyance, because the sensitive is in a normal state, not in trance. But there is a further stage, into which, indeed, Mr Wilkinson sometimes passes, in which there is a change of personality, and a spirit purports to speak or write with the medium's organs. There is nothing weird or uncanny in the procedure, nothing deathly or coma-like; the medium usually sits up and even walks about, though some trance mediums have to sit still and keep their eyes closed. I have had visits from many trance mediums; and most of them have failed to get anything evidential—which at least suggests their honesty, for they could easily have obtained *some* information about my deceased relatives. But the whole matter of trance control is a thorny problem. Indubitably, evidence of supernormal faculty is sometimes given in this state, but we of the S.P.R. are divided as to what the control really is. Some think it is a spirit, as claimed; others think it is a secondary personality of the medium, as in the remarkable case of split personality described in Dr Morton Prince's book *The Dissociation of a Personality*. Mrs Sidgwick, widow of the Professor and sister of Mr A. J. Balfour, has made a careful psychological study of the case of Mrs Piper, given in 657 pages of *Proceedings*, vol. 28, and her conclusion is that though telepathy from the dead is probably shown, and certainly some kind of supernormality, the controls themselves are dream-fragments of the medium's mind. I am not qualified to pronounce an opinion on Mrs Piper, not having met her; but as to the trance mediums I have experimented with, I incline to agree with Mrs Sidgwick. I think it may be a dodge of the subliminal to get the over-anxious normal consciousness temporarily out of the way. But this is a psychological detail, and a difficult one, requiring much further study. From the psychical research point of view Mrs Piper's case may be studied in *Proceedings*, vols. 6, 8, 13, 16, and a few of the later ones, or some idea of it can be got from Sir Oliver Lodge's *Survival of Man*. All the investigators were convinced of either telepathy or something more. Fraud was excluded by introducing sitters anonymously, Dr Hodgson himself introducing over 150 different people in this way, and taking careful notes. I have experimented similarly with Wilkinson, introducing people from distant places such as Middlesex and Northumberland as well as from towns nearer home, either under false names or with no names at all, and being present myself to take notes. Friends of mine have done the same thing. We were unanimously sceptical to start with, probably more sceptical than most of those who will read this paper, for we disbelieved in survival itself. We are now convinced that the fraud theory is out of the question, that at the very least a complicated theory of mind-reading—including the reading of the minds of distant and unknown persons—must be assumed if the theory of survival and communication is to be avoided.

Of late years there has been a great development in automatic writing among quite non-professional mediums—private people who are members of the S.P.R., as for instance the late Mrs Verrall, Classical Lecturer at Newnham—and some noteworthy evidence has been obtained. But it is too complex even to summarise here. It seems to be the work of Gurney, Hodgson, Myers, and Sidgwick, on the other side, for different messages have come through different sensitives, making sense when put together, and sense characteristic of these departed leaders. This had not been thought of, so far as we know, by any living person, and it seems to eliminate telepathy from the living, for the messages are not understood until the bits are pieced together. The evidence fills several volumes of our *Proceedings*, and students should read them carefully.

There are many other kinds of mediumship or psychic faculty, and many volumes are in existence on each phase; the library of the London Spiritualist Alliance contains about 3,000. I have read about 500 of them, and would not recommend anyone else to do the same. There is a great deal of rubbish among them, though they are not all rubbish. The reading I recommend is the *Proceedings* of the S.P.R., the writings of Sir William Barrett, Sir Oliver Lodge, Dr W. J. Crawford, and, above all, the great work of F. W. H. Myers, *Human Personality and Its Survival of Bodily Death*, in the original two-volume edition. The abridged one-volume edition omits many of the illustrative cases. I do not think that conviction is to be achieved by mere reading; books would never have convinced me. But careful reading is perhaps sufficient to lead a fairly tolerant mind to realise that there is something here which must not be dismissed off-hand; something which is worthy of investigation. That is as much as we expect. Sir Oliver Lodge often says that we shall do well if we succeed, in this generation, in modifying the psychological climate, creating an atmosphere more favourable to unprejudiced examination of the facts. We have no desire for revolutions; we want knowledge to grow slowly and surely. The S.P.R. has been in existence only thirty-seven years, and the subject is in its scientific infancy. Take the beginnings of any one science—say, Chemistry, dating it somewhat arbitrarily from Priestley or Dalton—and note what a little way discovery had gone in a like period. With increased numbers of workers the pace increases; but in every science the progress at first must be slow. In psychical research a good start has been made, and the investigators seem to be certainly on the track of something, whether their inferences are right in every detail or not. And every advance in science has extended our conceptions of this wonderful universe. The heavens declare the glory of God in a tremendously larger way than they did in the days of the old Ptolemaic astronomy, though man foolishly fought the Copernican idea because it seemed to lessen our dignity by making our earth a speck on the scale of creation instead of the central body thereof. So with all other phenomena, physical and psychical. We may be sure that all discovery will be real revelation. With this faith—a well-grounded faith—we need not fear advance.

RECENT CRITICISM

I add a few words, rather against my inclination, about recent criticism of a kind which is hardly worthy that name. Two books, one by Dr Mercier and one by Mr Edward Clodd, have had a certain popularity, mainly because they attacked, with a certain smartness of phrase, the book of a greater man. "Raymond" was being widely read and talked about, and its popularity secured some success for these hostile books. Curiously enough, even some of the clergy have quoted approvingly some of the arguments of these rationalists, no doubt much to the glee of Mr Clodd in particular. Now I have said before that instructed criticism is always welcome, for we may hope to learn something from it. But Dr Mercier, on his own statement, came new to the subject at the age of sixty-four, read *Raymond* and *The Survival of Man*, and immediately sat down to write a flippant book the publication of which we hope he now regrets. Not only had he never investigated for himself, but he was also ignorant of the work of the S.P.R.

As to Mr Clodd, his book is better-informed, though frequently unfair. For instance, in his references to me he is very careful to avoid any consideration of the strong parts of my case. Like the famous theological professor, he looks the difficulties boldly in the face—not *very* boldly—and passes on, without speaking to them. He has obviously read fairly widely, but where he does criticise in detail, he always seizes on weak points and quietly ignores the strong ones. As to personal investigation he is almost entirely without experience. He says he attended a séance about fifty years ago, but has forgotten most of what happened! He says this, with a momentary lapse from his usual cleverness—for it gives away his case—in a letter to the April (1918) *International Psychic Gazette*. In other words, he poses as an authority on a branch of science of which he has no first-hand knowledge. He criticises and dismisses airily the opinions and investigations of those who have worked at the subject for ten, twenty, thirty, or forty years; for it is over forty years since Sir William Barrett brought his experiments in telepathy before the British Association. Mr Clodd is a Rationalist, and knows without investigation that these things cannot be. He is as *à prioristic* as a medieval Schoolman, in spite of his scientific pose. And his prejudices unfortunately prevent him from seeking and studying the facts which might lead him to other conclusions.

34

I have not said anything about the S.P.R. itself, but may here add a few remarks. Says its official leaflet: "The aim of the Society is to approach these various problems without prejudice or prepossession of any kind, and in the same spirit of exact and unimpassioned inquiry which has enabled Science to solve so many problems, once not less obscure nor less hotly debated.... Membership of the Society does not imply the acceptance of any particular explanation of the phenomena investigated, nor any belief as to the operation, in the physical world, of forces other than those recognised by Physical Science". In other words, the Society has no creed, except that the subject is worth investigating.

The Society has well over 1,000 members, and is growing steadily. It includes many famous men in all walks of life, and indeed its membership list has been said to contain more well-known names than any other scientific society except the Royal Society itself. Among the Vice-presidents are the Right Honourables A. J. and G. W. Balfour, Sir William Barrett, Sir Oliver Lodge, the late Bishop Boyd-Carpenter and the late Sir William Crookes. The President for the current year is Lord Rayleigh, probably the greatest mathematical physicist now living.[5] The President of the Royal Society (Sir J. J. Thomson) is a member, also Professor Henri Bergson of Paris, Dr L. P. Jacks (editor of *The Hibbert Journal*) and innumerable other scientists and scholars whose names are known to everyone.

Finally let me assure you that the S.P.R. is so conservative and suspicious that admission is almost as difficult to obtain as membership of a high-class London club. It is extremely anxious to keep out cranks and emotional people of all sorts, and it requires any applicant to be vouched for as suitable by two existing members; and each application is separately considered by

---

[5] Lord Rayleigh's lamented death has since occurred, July, 1919.

the Council. The result is a level-headed lot of members, and the maintenance of a sane and scientific attitude and management.

From the philosophic side it is sometimes urged that we cannot reason from the phenomenal to the noumenal, from the world of appearance to the world of reality; that consequently nothing happening in the material world can prove the existence of a spiritual one. But this is easily answered. We cheerfully agree, with Kant, that a spiritual world cannot be proved coercively and in such knock-down fashion that belief cannot be avoided. But it can be proved in the same way and to the same extent as many other things which we believe and find ourselves justified in believing. For instance, atoms and electrons and the Ether of Space are not phenomenal; no one has ever seen or heard or felt or smelt them; but we infer their real existence from the behaviour of the matter which does affect our senses. Again: we cannot *prove* to ourselves that other human beings exist, or even that an external world exists; my experience may be a huge subjective hallucination. If I were reading this paper I should not be able to prove to myself that any other mind was present. Looking around, I should receive certain impressions—sensations of sight—and I should call certain aggregations of these the physical bodies of beings like myself. From the similarity of their structure and behaviour to the structure and behaviour of my own body, I should infer that they have got minds somehow associated with them, as my mind is associated with my body. But you could not prove it to me. If you got angry with my obstinacy, and knocked me down, I should experience painful sensations, but the existence of a mind external to me—and an angry one—would still be a matter of inference only. But we find that the inference is justified. We find that it "works," and social life is possible. For the purposes, then, both of science and of ordinary life, we do reason from phenomenon to noumenon, from appearance to reality, from attribute to substance; and our reasoning justifies itself. I affirm, therefore, that the kind of proof which we as psychical researchers put forward for the existence of and

36

communication from discarnate minds, is philosophically the same kind as the proof we have of the existence of incarnate minds. If a short and clear exposition of the point is required, free from any psychical-research bias, I may refer inquirers to the chapter on the Psychological Theory of an External World in J. S. Mill's *Examination of Sir William Hamilton's Philosophy.* Our evidence may be insufficient to justify belief—in the opinion of many, it is—and I blame no one for disbelieving; but it is evidence. And if it sufficiently accumulates and improves in quality, it may amount to a degree of proof at least comparable with that concerning electrons, which are now accepted as real by all physicists.

One or two difficulties may here be briefly referred to:

I. The appearance in Mrs Piper's script of such obvious dream-stuff as messages from Homer, Ulysses, and Telemachus! These are of course absurdities, and no psychical researcher regards them as anything else. But they are no more absurd than many of our own dreams, and we must remember that automatic writing comes from the dream-strata of the medium's mind, these strata seeming to lie *between* our normal consciousness and the spiritual world. Consequently messages which really seem to come from beyond: *i.e.,* which are evidential—are often mixed with subliminal matter from the medium's mind. As a communicator once said: "The medium's dreams get in my way." All this has to be allowed for, but in good mediums there is not much of it. In my friend Wilkinson's case there is none, for he can distinguish. In Mrs Piper's case there is a little, but it does not invalidate the huge mass of real evidence that has come. And it at least testifies to her honesty, for no medium would pretend to get messages from people whom everyone knows to be mythical—messages which are indeed comic and therefore enable opponents to score points with the general public by obvious witticisms.

Huxley is often referred to, as having wisely declined to investigate, knowing beforehand that it was all nonsense. Huxley was busy with his own work, and, believing *à priori* that alleged psychical phenomena were either fraud or self-delusion, naturally declined to give any time to them. We need not regret his decision, for he was doing work that was more important than psychical investigation would have been, just then. But he was wrong in his *à priori* belief, or rather unbelief. He had never seen any of these phenomena, but that did not prove that they did not happen. A native of mid-Africa may never have seen snow, but that does not prove that no snow exists.

And it happens that the Dialectical Society went on with its task, appointing committees which investigated without any paid medium. The majority of the investigators were utterly sceptical at first; they were practically all convinced at the finish. I state this merely as a fact, not as a specially important fact; for I find that beginners, when suddenly faced with striking phenomena, are liable to go from the extreme of unbelief to an extreme of belief. When one's materialistic scheme is exploded, there seems no criterion left, and anything may happen. It usually takes an investigator a year or two to adjust himself and to learn to follow the evidence and not overshoot it.

Some people say: "But if communication is possible, why cannot *I* communicate direct with my own departed loved ones?" The question is seen on reflection, however, to be easily answered. In the first place, we cannot communicate direct even with our friends in the next town; we have to get the help of postmen or telegraph clerks and the like. It is therefore not at all surprising that an intermediary is needed when they are removed further from our conditions. Probably all of us have germs of psychic faculty—though I have not yet discovered any in myself—somewhat as we can all play or sing a little; but the Paderewskis and Carusos are few. Similarly with psychic faculty. Few have enough of it to communicate for themselves. On the other hand, it is much commoner than Carusos are; but of course, when it occurs in a private person, that person does not advertise the fact. Outsiders would either scoff, or say "lunacy", or crowd round asking for "sittings", out of curiosity. Consequently only sympathetic intimates are told, or people who, like myself, are known to be sympathetic investigators. Some of the most remarkable sensitives in England at the present day are of this private kind—people of education and position—and they are not even spiritualists in the sense of belonging to the spiritualist sect. They are of various religious persuasions, and belong mostly to rather orthodox bodies. There is nothing of the crank about them; they are not Theosophists or Christian Scientists or adherents of any other of what the sergeant called "fancy religions." I may say that the most extraordinary experiences I have ever had have been with a psychic of this kind. I have not alluded to these experiences in my paper, because the matter is private. But I just mention these things because I find that psychic faculties are more common than I once thought, and a sympathetic minister could probably hear of private cases if he let his sympathy and interest be known. But of course, if he is known to have condemned the whole thing as Satanic—as Father Bernard Vaughan does—or as lunacy, people with psychic experiences will take very good care not to tell him about them.

As to details about the nature of the after-life, I have no dogmatic opinions to offer. Probably it is impossible for those over there to describe their experience adequately, in our earthly terms. Such information as we get must be largely symbolical, as when mediums describe a specially good deceased person as surrounded with radiance. I have several times noticed that the relative "brightness" or "radiance" of a spirit, as described by the medium, has correctly indicated that spirit's character, though the medium had no normal knowledge whatever of either the person's character or even existence. But though our information must probably be mainly symbolical, I think we are justified in believing that we begin the next stage pretty nearly where we leave off here. There is no sudden jump to unalloyed bliss for even such good people as you, no sudden plunge to everlasting woe even for sinners like me. This, I admit, is not in accordance with what I used to hear from the pulpit twenty years ago. But it agrees with what I read now of the opinions of such men as the Bishop of London and Dr J. D. Jones; and other clerical writers, such as Canon Storr in his *Christianity and Immortality* and Dr Paterson Smyth in his excellent *Gospel of the Hereafter* take the same view. Our modern moral sense refuses to believe that a good God will sentence any creature to everlasting pain; and although it may be contended that man has free-will and is therefore the arbiter of his own fate, it still remains that God gave him that freedom, and therefore still bears the ultimate responsibility. To retain belief in a God who can be loved and worshipped, I at least must disbelieve in everlasting pain for anyone.

And, added to this moral revolt, there has come a war in which millions of young men have died before their natural time. These young fellows, we feel, are at least in most cases neither good enough for heaven nor bad enough for hell. The sensible supposition seems to be—and it is borne out by psychical facts— that they have gone on to the next stage of life, which to most or all of them is an improvement; that they are busy and happy there; that they are still more or less interested in and cognisant of our affairs; that they will come to meet their loved ones when *they* cross over—of this I have had much evidence—and that they and humanity as a whole are travelling on an upward path toward some goal at present inconceivable to our small and flesh-bound souls.

Some people have objected that psychical research will substitute knowledge for faith. This is surely a curious objection, and few will advance it. The earth is the Lord's and the fulness thereof, and my belief is that He wants us to learn all we can about His handiwork. Nature is a book given to us by our Father, for our good; study of it is a duty, neglect of it is unfilial and wrong.

Psychical research studies its own particular facts in nature, and is thus trying to learn a little more of God's mind. It is not we, but those who oppose us, who are irreligious.

And as to this matter of faith; well, after we have learnt all we can, there will still be plenty of scope left for the exercise of faith in general, for our knowledge will always be surrounded by regions of the unknown. If anyone says that psychical research antagonises *Christian* faith, I say most emphatically that on the contrary it *supports* it. Christianity was based on a Fact: the Resurrection and Appearances of Jesus. Psychical-research facts are rendering that event credible to many who have disbelieved it. Myers says that in consequence of our evidence, everyone will believe, a century hence, in that Resurrection; whereas, in default of our evidence, a century hence no one would have believed it. And to him, personally, psychical research brought back the Christian faith which he had lost.

I hope that the facts and inferences which I have very sketchily put before you will have made it clear that there is some reality in the subject-matter of our investigations, and that these latter powerfully support a religious view of the universe. I believe that we are giving materialism its death-blow; hence the wild antagonism of such well-meaning but belated writers as Mr Clodd. But we are not ourselves religious teachers. That is your domain. You will use our work and its results, as you use the work and results of other labourers in the scientific vineyard. And I think you will find ours specially helpful.

THE EVOLUTION OF A PSYCHICAL RESEARCHER

Probably few of us keep a diary nowadays. I don't. But I somehow got into the habit, soon after I became interested in psychical things, of jotting down in a notebook the conclusions at which I had arrived—or the almost complete puzzlement in which I found myself, as the case might be. Glancing recently through these records of my pilgrimage, it seemed to me that a sketch of it might be of some interest or amusement to others.

Professor William James says in his *Talks to Teachers* that it is very difficult for most people to accept any new truth after the age of thirty; and that indeed old-fogeyism may be said to begin at twenty-five. It is perhaps therefore not surprising that, coming fresh to the subject at thirty-two—in 1905—I found the struggle to psychical truth a very long and arduous affair. Having been brought up on the ministrations of a hell-fire-preaching Nonconformist pastor whose theology made me into a very vigorous Huxleyan agnostic, I was biased against anything that savoured of "religion," and moreover "spiritualism" was unscientific and absurd. So I thought, in my ignorance; for I knew nothing whatever of the evidence on which spiritualistic beliefs are based.

However, I fortunately ran up against hard facts which soon cured me of negative dogmatism. I became acquainted with a medium who satisfied me that she could diagnose disease, or rather her medical "control" could, from a lock of the patient's hair; and this without any information whatever being given. Also that the diagnosis often went beyond the knowledge of the sitter, thus excluding telepathy from anyone present or near. But this did not prove that the control was a spirit, so I turned to other investigations.

First, I set myself to "read up". I feel sure that this is the best course for beginners to adopt, after once achieving real open-mindedness. It enables one to investigate with proper scientific care when opportunity arises, and with much better chance of securing good evidence. Without this preparation, an investigator has little idea how to handle that delicate machine called a medium, and indeed no amount of reading will entirely equip the experimenter, for there are many things which only experience can teach. Also, without this preparation, the investigator will be liable either to give things away by talking too much, or will create an atmosphere of suspicion and discomfort by being too secretive. It takes some practice to achieve an open and friendly manner while never losing sight of the importance of imparting no information that would spoil possible evidence. This of course is desirable from the medium's point of view as well as that of the sitter. It is hard on a medium if, for example, a really supernormally-got name does not count because the sitter himself had let it slip.

I think my reading began with *Light* and some of Mr E. W. Wallis's books, but I soon found my way to the *Proceedings of the Society for Psychical Research*, and recognised that here was what I was seeking. I cannot sufficiently express my admiration, which is as great as ever, for such masterly pieces of evidence as, for instance, Dr Hodgson's account of sittings with Mrs Piper, in volume 13. If we were perfectly logical beings, without prejudice, that account ought to convince anybody; certainly it ought to convince the reader of the operation of *something* supernormal, and it ought to go a long way towards excluding telepathic theories and rendering the spirit explanation the most reasonable one. But we are not logical beings. We require to be battered for a long time by fact after fact before we will admit a new conclusion. I remember saying, as indeed I noted down in the diary mentioned, that a few of these volumes, with Myers's *Human Personality*, left me in the curious position of being able to say that, though I was not convinced, I felt that logically I ought to be, for the evidence seemed irrefragable. Then I read Crookes' *Researches in the Phenomena of Spiritualism*, and my logical agreement was accentuated, for Sir William Crookes was my scientific Pope, in consequence of my having worked from his chemical writings, and having an immense admiration for his mind and method. But my actual inner conviction was not much changed. Kant says somewhere that we may test the strength of our beliefs by asking ourselves what we would bet on them. At this point I had not got to the stage of being prepared to bet much on the truth of the survival of human beings or the possibility of communicating with them if they did survive. I thought the case was logically proved, but I didn't feel it in my bones, as the phrase goes. For this, personal experience is necessary; at least it is for an old fogey of over thirty, with my particular build of mind.

And I was fortunately able to get this experience. One of the two best-known mediums in the North of England, Mr A. Wilkinson, happened to live only a few miles away, though he was and is generally away from home, speaking for spiritualist societies from Aberdeen to Exeter, and being booked over a year ahead. However, I was able to get an introduction to him through friends who also carried out investigations with him (described in my *New Evidences in Psychical Research*), and since then, with intermissions due mainly to ill-health, I have had friendly sittings with him continuously. To him I owe my real convictions, and for this I cannot adequately thank him. Without his kindness I could never have achieved certainty; for owing to a damaged heart I could not get about to interview mediums, and there was no other medium within reasonable distance. Besides, Mr Wilkinson has stretched a point in my case, for he does not give private sittings, preferring to confine himself to platform work; and I suppose he makes an exception in my case in view of my inability. I here once more thank him for all he has done for me.

44

At my first sitting with him he described and named my mother and other relatives, whom he saw apparently with me. I had no reason to believe that he had any normal knowledge of these people; certainly I had never mentioned them to him, and it was in the last degree unlikely that anyone else had. My mother had been dead twenty-two years, and was not at all a prominent person. Moreover, he got by automatic writing a signed message from her, giving the name of the house in which we lived at the time of her death, but which we had left eleven years later. This seemed to be given by way of a test. At later sittings my father and other relatives manifested, with names and identifying detail, and the proof began to be almost coercive. The evidence went beyond any possibility of the medium's normal knowledge, and was characteristic of the different communicators in all sorts of subtle ways. Telepathy alone remained as a possible alternative to the spirit explanation. Then came a peculiar phase, as if there were a definite plan on the part of some of my friends on the other side for the purpose of utterly convincing me by bringing evidence which could not possibly be accounted for by any supposition of a reading of my own mind. A spirit friend of mine would turn up, bringing with him a spirit whom I had never heard of, and saying that he was a friend of his; and on inquiry I would find that it was so—and sometimes it needed a great deal of inquiry, which made it all the better evidence, for it showed how difficult it would have been for the medium to obtain the information; though indeed at this stage the evidence had forced me past crude suspicions of that sort. On other occasions unknown spirits would appear, and I would find that they belonged to the last visitor I had had. Several incidents of this kind are described in my book *Psychical Investigations*. After some years of this kind of experience I became fully satisfied that the spirit explanation was the only reasonable one. Some writers, like Miss Dougall in a recent volume of essays called *Immortality*, invent a complicated hypothesis according to which my mind photographs the mind of a visitor and the medium on his next visit develops and reads off the photograph; but I confess that my credulity does not stand the strain put upon it by such a hypothesis. Besides, I have lately had—as if to get round even such tortured theories as this—evidence giving details which have not been known to any person I have ever met. I was told to write to a certain friend of mine, father of the ostensible communicator. The facts were unknown even to him, but he was able to verify them completely; and they were characteristic and evidential of the identity of the ostensible communicator.

If all my results were of the kind I have had through Mr Wilkinson the case would, for me, be so utterly and overwhelmingly proved that doubt would be absurd. But this is too much to expect. I have had many other mediums here, with varying success, but nothing approaching Mr Wilkinson's. In many cases it is fairly obvious that the medium's subliminal—or the control's imagination—has been doing part of the business, no doubt unknown to the medium's normal consciousness. But in no case have I had any indication of fraud. This seems sufficient answer to Mr Edward Clodd's credulous acceptance of the theory of a Blue-Book and inquiry system which enables mediums to post themselves up about likely sitters. It would be the easiest thing in the world for an imitation medium to learn enough about me to give what would seem on the face of it a fairly "good" sitting. But this is never the case. Either the medium fails or he is so successful that normal knowledge is ruled out. On Mr Clodd's theory, I ought to have neither of these extremes; I ought to have no failures, and no results going beyond what inquiry could produce. But I need not labour this point, for Mr Clodd has recently confessed his almost absurd innocence of any first-hand experience. In a letter to the *International Psychic Gazette* for April, 1918, he said he had been to a sitting about fifty years ago, but he does not remember much about what happened! Yet he sets up as an authority on this branch of experimental science! It is like someone writing on chemistry after being in a laboratory once, fifty years ago.

Some of my most curious experiences, concerning which I have not yet published anything in detail, have been in connexion with crystal vision. I happen to know a sensitive—not a professional medium or even a spiritualist—who has physical-phenomena powers of very unusual and indeed probably unique type. Not only can she see in the crystal and get evidential messages by writing seen therein, but the writing or pictures are visible to anyone present. I have seen them myself. As many as six people at a time, myself among them, have seen the same thing, and not one of the six was of suggestible type or had had any hallucinations. All were middle-aged, except one young lieutenant, and we were indeed a rather exceptionally un-neurotic and stodgy lot. But though the things seem objective—I am going to try to photograph them, also the sensitive, in the hope of confirming the Crewe phenomena—they are somehow more or less influenced by the sensitive's own mind, without her conscious knowledge; for, *e.g.*, in one message, purporting to come from my father, I was addressed as Arthur, a name which would be natural to the medium who knows me mostly from printed matter and a few letters, but which is entirely inappropriate in relation to my father. Yet a good deal of evidence of identity has come through this sensitive, and this "mixture" does not invalidate the case. Again, a queer feature of this sensitive's powers is that lost objects are frequently found as a result of instructions given in the crystal; and in many of these cases it seems certain that the position of the lost object could not have been known to any incarnate mind, or of course it would not have been left there. In one case it was a valuable ruby; in several others it was Treasury notes. This sensitive also is a medium for very good raps, which all present can hear quite distinctly and which show intelligence, answering questions and so forth.

I have therefore reached the conviction that human survival is a fact, that the life over there is something like an improved version of the present one, and—a comforting thought, supported by much of my evidence—that we are met at death by those who have gone before. Some of my more mystical friends, who have not needed such prolonged jolting to get them out of materialistic grooves, are rather bored with me for dwelling so much on the evidence and on the nature of the next state. They call it "merely astral"; as for them, their minds soar in higher flights. One friend, a sort of radical High Churchman, said to me some time ago that he was "not interested in the intermediate state". But I rather think that he will have to be. I may be wrong, but I suspect that, whether they like it or not, these good people will have to go through the intermediate state before they get anywhere else. Good though they are, I do not believe they are good enough for unalloyed bliss or union with the Godhead. Such sudden jumps do not happen. Progress is gradual. Indeed, I have noticed lately that my High Churchman friend has shown much more interest in these merely psychical things. Perhaps he thinks he had better turn back and make sure of the next state and its nature, perceiving that it is a necessary bridge or "tarrying-place" (which is the alternative reading for the "mansions" of our Father's house) on the way to the heaven which he quite rightly aims at.

As to the future of psychical science and opinion, I feel sure that great things are now ahead. The war, with the terrible amount of mourning it entails, has quickened interest in the subject, and for millions of people the question of survival and the next state has become an urgent and abiding one. Their interest, instead of being almost wholly on this side, is very largely over there, whither their loved ones have gone. Similarly with the soldiers who have come safely through the war. All have lost friends, all have faced the possibility of sudden or slow and painful death. And probably all young people at present, and most adults, have out-grown the crude beliefs of last century's orthodoxy with its everlasting hell, and are ready for a more rational system. This is being supplied, backed by scientific proof, by psychical research and scientific spiritualism. It seems likely that the religion of the best minds for the next half-century or so, and perhaps onward, will be something like that which Myers came to hold in his later years. It does not much matter whether the spiritualist sect grows as an institution or not. Many people will accept its main belief without feeling it necessary to leave the communion to which they already belong. It seems certain that the idea itself will be the ruling idea in many minds for a long time, and no doubt psychic faculty will become much more common, for thousands are now trying to develop it who never cared to try before. Quite possibly the effort on both sides of the veil, in consequence of so many premature deaths, may bring about a closer communion between the two sides than has ever been known hitherto. A great lift-up of earthly thought would be the result, a perhaps final emergence from the chrysalis stage of materialism; and we shall then be near the time when, as the inspired Milton makes his Raphael say:

"Your bodies may at last turn all to spirit, Improved by tract of time, and winged ascend Ethereal, as we, or may, at choice, Here or in heavenly Paradises dwell."

DO MIRACLES HAPPEN?

Mr G. K. Chesterton, with true journalistic instinct, recently stimulated public interest in himself and other worthy things by engineering a discussion on "Do Miracles Happen?" The debate furnished an opportunity of harmlessly letting off steam, but apparently each disputant "was of his own opinion still" at the finish; though some of the newspapers thought that the affirmative was proved, not by argument, but by the actual occurrence of a miracle at the meeting—for Mr Bernard Shaw was present, but remained silent! Joking apart, however, these discussions are usually rendered nugatory by each debater attaching a different meaning to the word. To one of them, a "miracle" involves the action of some non-human mind; to others it is only a "wonderful" occurrence, which is the strictly etymological meaning. It is only in the latter sense that orthodox science has anything to say on the subject.

David Hume, in the most famous of his essays, says that a miracle is "a violation of the laws of nature", which laws a "firm and unalterable experience has established". A century later, Matthew Arnold disposed of the question in an even shorter manner. "Miracles do not happen", said he, in the preface to *Literature and Dogma*. Modern science has, speaking generally, concurred.

But the two statements are not very satisfactory. It is true, no doubt, that miracles did not enter into the experience of David Hume and Matthew Arnold; but this does not prove that they have never entered into the experience of anybody else. If I must disbelieve all assertions concerning phenomena which I have not personally observed, I must deny that the sun can ever be north at mid-day, as indeed the Greeks did (according to Herodotus), when the circumnavigators of Africa came back with their story. But if I do, I shall be wrong. (*Histories*, book iv, "I for my part do not believe them", says even this romantic historian.)

It is as unsafe to reject all human testimony to the marvellous as it is to accept it all without question. The modern mind has gone to the negative extreme, as the medieval mind went to the other. Take for instance the twenty-five thousand Lives of the Saints in the great Bollandist collection. They are full of miracles, of most incredible kinds; yet in those days the accounts caused no astonishment. There was no organised knowledge of nature, outside the narrow orbit of daily life—and how narrow that was, we with our facile means of communication and travel can hardly realise. Consequently there was little or no conception of law or orderliness in nature, and therefore no criterion by which to test stories of unusual occurrences. Anything might happen; there was no apparent reason why it shouldn't. One saint having retired into the desert to lead a life of mortification, the birds daily brought him food sufficient for his wants; and when a brother joined him they doubled the supply. When the saint died, two lions came and dug his grave, uttered a howl of mourning over his body, and knelt to beg a blessing from the survivor. (Cf. the curious story of St Francis taming "Brother Wolf", of Gubbio, in chapter 21 of the *Fioretti.*) The innumerable miracles in the *Little Flowers* and *Life of St Francis* are repeated in countless other lives; saints are lifted across rivers by angels, they preach to the fishes, who swarm to the shore to listen, they are visited by the Virgin, are lifted up in the air and suspended there for twelve hours while in ecstasy they perceive the inner mystery of the Most Blessed Trinity. Almost every town in Europe could produce its relic which has produced its miraculous cures, or its image that had opened or shut its eyes, or bowed its head to a worshipper. The Virgin of the Pillar, at Saragossa, restored a worshipper's leg that had been amputated. This is regarded by Spanish theologians as specially well attested. There is a picture of it in the Cathedral at Saragossa. (Lecky, *Rise and Influence of Rationalism in Europe*, vol. I, page 141.) The saints were seen fighting for the Christian army, when the latter battled with the infidel. In medieval times this kind of thing was accepted without question and without surprise.

About the end of the twelfth century there came a change. The human mind began to awake from its long lethargy; began to writhe and struggle against the dead hand of authority which held it down. The Crusades, as Guizot shows, had much to do with the rise of the new spirit, by causing educative contact with a high Saracenic civilization. Men began to wonder and to think. Heresy inevitably appeared, and became rife. In 1208 Innocent III established the Inquisition, but failed to strangle the infant Hercules. In 1209 began the massacre of the Albigenses, which continued more or less for about fifty years, the deaths being at least scores of thousands; but the blood of the martyrs was the seed of further freedom and enlightenment. Nature began to be studied, in however rudimentary a way, by Roger Bacon and his brother alchemists. The Reformation came, weakening ecclesiastical authority still further by dividing the dogmatic forces into two hostile camps, and thus giving science its chance. Galileo appeared, and did his work, though with many waverings, for Paul V and Urban VIII kept successively a heavy hand on him; he was imprisoned at seventy, when in failing health, and, some think, tortured—though this is uncertain, and his famous *e pur si muove* is probably mythical. More important still, Francis Bacon, teaching with enthusiasm the method of observation and experiment. The conception of law, of rationality and regularity in nature, emerged; Kepler and Newton laid down the ground plan of the universe, evolving the formulæ which express the facts of molar motion. Uniformity in geology was shown by Lyell, while Darwin and his followers carried law into biological evolution. Then man became swelled-headed; became intoxicated with his successes. It had already been so with Hume, and it became more so with his disciples. Man treated his own limited experience as a criterion, and denied what was not represented by something similar therein. Especially was this the case when alleged facts had any connection with religion. Religion had tried to exterminate science, and it was natural enough that, in revenge, science should be hostile to anything associated with religion. Consequently, the scientific man flatly denied miracles, not only such stories as the rib of Adam and the talking serpent (concerning which even a church father like Origen had made merry in Gnostic days fifteen hundred years before), but also the healing miracles of Jesus, which to us are now beginning to look possible enough.

This negative dogmatism is as regrettable as the positive variety. It is not scientific. Science stands for a method, not for a dogma. It observes, experiments, and infers; but it makes no claim to the possession of absolute truth. A genuine science, confronted with allegations of unusual facts, neither believes nor disbelieves. It investigates. The solution of the problem is simply a question of evidence. Huxley in his little book *Hume*, and J. S. Mill in his *Essays on Religion*, made short work of the "impossibility" attitude. Says the former in *Science and Christian Tradition*, page 197:

"Strictly speaking, I am unaware of anything that has a right to the title of an impossibility, except a contradiction in terms. There are impossibilities logical, but none natural. A 'round square', a 'present past', 'two parallel lines that intersect', are impossibilities, because the ideas denoted by the predicates round, present, intersect, are contradictory of the ideas denoted by the subjects square, past, parallel. But walking on water, or turning water into wine, are plainly not impossibilities in this sense".

No alleged occurrence can be ruled out as impossible, then, unless the statement is self-contradictory. Difficulty of belief is no reason. It was found difficult to believe in Antipodes; if there were people on the under side of the earth, "they would fall off". But the advance of knowledge made it not only credible but quite comprehensible. People stick on, all over the earth, because the earth attracts them more powerfully than anything else does. Similarly with some miracles. They may seem much more credible and comprehensible when we have learned more. Indeed, the wonders of wireless telegraphy, radio-activity, and aviation are intrinsically as miraculous as many of the stories in the world's sacred writings.

This is not saying, however, that we are to believe the latter *en bloc.* They must be taken individually, and believed or disbelieved according to the evidence and according to the antecedent probability or improbability. The standing still of the sun (*Joshua*, x) does not seem credible to the scientific mind which knows that the earth is spinning at the equator at the rate of one thousand miles an hour and that any sudden interference with that rotation would send it to smithereens, with all the creatures on its surface. Of course, a Being who could stop its rotation could perhaps also prevent it from flying to smithereens; but we have to extend the miracle in so many entirely hypothetical ways that the whole thing becomes too dubious for acceptance. It is simpler to look on the story as a myth.

But such things as the clairvoyance of Samuel (I *Samuel,* x), and even the Woman of Endor story, are quite in line with what psychical research is now establishing. And the healing miracles of Jesus are paralleled, in kind if not in degree, by innumerable "suggestive therapeutic" doctors. Shell-shock blindness and paralysis are cured at Seale Hayne Hospital and elsewhere in very "miraculous" fashion. And turning water into wine is not more wonderful than turning radium into helium, and helium into lead, which nature is now doing before our eyes. These things, therefore, have become credible, if the evidence is good enough. Whether evidence nineteen hundred years old can be good enough to take as the basis of serious belief is another matter. Scientific method insists on a high standard of evidence. We must be honest with ourselves, and not believe unless the evidence satisfies our intellectual requirements. But the modern and wise tendency is to regard religion as an attitude rather than as a belief or system of beliefs. It does not stand or fall with the miracle-stories.

THE TRUTH ABOUT TELEPATHY

The amount of nonsense that is talked, and apparently widely believed, about telepathy, is almost enough to make one wish that the phenomenon had not been discovered, or the word invented. Without any adequate basis of real knowledge, the "man in the street" seems to be accepting the idea of thought-transference as an incontrovertible fact, like wireless telegraphy—which latter is responsible for a good deal of easy credence accorded to the former, both seeming equally wonderful. But the analogy is a false one. There is a great deal of difference between the two. In wireless telegraphy we understand the process: it is a shaking of the ether into pulses or waves, which act on the coherer in a perfectly definite way and are measurable. But in spite of much loose talk about "brain-waves", the fact is that we know of no such thing. Indeed, there is reason to believe that telepathy, if it is a fact at all—and I believe it is—may turn out to be a process of a different kind, the nature of which is at present unknown. For one thing, it does not seem to conform to physical laws. If it were an affair of ripples in the ether—like wireless telegraphy—the strength of impact would vary in inverse ratio with the square of the distance. The influence would weaken at a known rate, as more and more distance intervened between sender and recipient. And this, in many cases at least, is not found to be so, consequently Mr Gerald Balfour and other leading members of the Society for Psychical Research incline to the opinion that the transmission is not a physical process, but takes place in the spiritual world.

I have said that I believe in telepathy, yet I have deprecated too-ready credence. What, then, are the facts?

The first attempt at serious investigation of alleged supernormal phenomena by an organised body of qualified observers was made by the London Society for Psychical Research, which was founded in 1882 by Henry Sidgwick (Professor of Moral

Philosophy at Cambridge), F. W. H. Myers and Edmund Gurney (Fellows of Trinity), W. F. Barrett (Professor of Experimental Physics at Dublin, and now Sir William), and a few friends. The membership grew, and the list now includes the most famous scientific names throughout the civilised world. In point of prestige, the society is one of the strongest in existence.

The first important work undertaken was the collection of a large number of cases of apparition, etc., in which there seemed to be some supernormal agency at work, conveying knowledge; as in the case of Lord Brougham, who saw an apparition of his friend at the moment of the latter's death. The results of this investigation were embodied in the two stout volumes called *Phantasms of the Living* (now out of print, but an abridged one-volume edition has recently been edited by Mrs Sidgwick (Kegan Paul, Trench, Trubner & Co., Ltd., 1919), and in Vol. x. of the *Proceedings* of the Society. As the outcome of this arduous investigation, involving the collection and consideration of about 17,000 cases and extending over several years of time, the committee made the cautious but memorable statement that "Between deaths and apparitions of the dying person a connexion exists which is not due to chance alone". This guarded statement was carefully worded in order to avoid committing the society to any definite (*e.g.* spiritualistic) interpretation. Some of the apparitions occurred within twelve hours before the death, some at the time of death, and some a few hours afterwards. But these latter of course do not prove "spirit-agency"—though indeed sometimes they seem to render it probable—for the telepathic impulse or thought may have been sent out by the dying person, remaining latent—so to speak—until the percipient happened to be in a sufficiently passive and receptive state to "take it in".

Definite experimentation was also made, of various kinds, *e.g.,* one person would be shown a card or diagram, and another (blindfolded) would maintain a passive mind, saying aloud what ideas "came into his head". Some of these experiments—which are still required and should be tried by those interested in the subject—indicated that the concentration of A's mind did indeed sometimes produce a reverberation in the mind of B. In a series conducted by Sir Oliver Lodge, the odds against the successes being due to chance can be mathematically shown to be ten millions to one.

For this new fact or agency, Mr Myers invented the word "telepathy" (Greek *tele*, at a distance, and *pathein*, to feel), and defined it as "communication of impressions of any kind from one mind to another, independently of the recognised channels of sense".

But I wish to say, and to emphasise the statement, that this transmission, though regarded as highly probable by many acute minds, cannot yet be regarded as unquestionably proved, still less as occurring in a common or frequent way. We have all of us known somebody who claimed to be able to make people turn round in church or in the street by "willing" them, but usually these claims cannot be substantiated. It is difficult to eliminate chance coincidence. And the folks who lay claim to these powers are usually of a mystery-loving, inaccurate build of mind, and therefore very unsafe guides. Moreover, how many times have they "willed" without result?

One reason why I deprecate easy credence, leaning to the sceptical side though believing that the thing sometimes happens, is, that there is danger of a return to superstition, if belief outruns the evidence. If the popular mind gets the notion that telepathy is more or less a constant occurrence—that mind can influence mind whenever it likes—there is a possibility of a return to the witchcraft belief which resulted in so many poor old women being burnt at the stake in the seventeenth century. I prefer excessive disbelief to excessive credulity in these things; it at least does not burn old women because they have a squint and a black cat and a grievance against someone who happens to have fallen ill. Unbalanced minds are very ready to believe that someone is influencing them. I have received quite a number of letters from people (not spiritualists) who, knowing of my interest in these matters, got it into their foolish heads that I was trying some sort of telepathic black magic on them. I had not even been thinking about them. It was entirely their own imagination. One of these people is now in an asylum. I think she would probably have become insane in any case—if not on this, then on some other subject—but these incidents almost make me wish that we could confine the investigation and discussion of the subject to our own circle or society until education has developed more balanced judgment in the masses. But of course such a restriction is impossible. The daily press and the sensational novelists have got hold of the idea. We must counteract the sensational exaggerations, which have such a bad effect on unbalanced minds, by stating the bare, hard facts. Here, as elsewhere, a little knowledge is a dangerous thing. It is the half-informed people who are endangered. The remedy is more knowledge. Let them learn that, though there is reason to believe that under certain conditions telepathy is possible and real, there is nevertheless no scientific evidence for anything in the nature of "bewitching", or telepathy of maleficent kind. This cannot be too strongly insisted on. Let us follow the facts with an open mind, but let us be careful not to rush beyond them into superstition.

THE TRUTH ABOUT HYPNOTISM

Various popular novelists, such as George Du Maurier in *Trilby*, and E. F. Benson in *The Image in the Sand*, have taken advantage of the possibilities which hypnotic marvels offer to the sensational writer, and have put into circulation a variety of exaggerated ideas. This is regrettable. Of course the novelist can choose his subject, and can treat it as he likes; it is the public's fault if it takes fiction for fact, or allows its notions of fact to be coloured or in any way influenced by what is avowedly no more than fiction.

But it is certain that it is thus influenced. It is therefore desirable that the public should be told from time to time exactly what the scientific position is—what the conclusions are, of those who are studying the subject in a proper scientific spirit, with no aim save the finding of truth. This will at least enable the public to discriminate between fact and fiction, if it wants to.

No doubt the phenomena in question have been often discovered, forgotten, and rediscovered; but in modern times the movement dates from Mesmer. Friedrich Anton Mesmer was born about 1733 or 1734. In 1766 he took his doctor's degree at Vienna, but did not come into public notice until 1773. In that year he employed in the treatment of patients certain magnetic plates, the invention of Father Hell, a Jesuit, professor of astronomy at Vienna.

Further experiments led him to believe that the human body is a kind of magnet; and that its effluent forces could be employed, like those of the metal plates, in the cure of disease. Between 1773 and 1778 he travelled extensively in Europe, with a view to making his discoveries better known. Also he sent an account of his system to the principal learned bodies of Europe, including the Royal Society of London, the Academy of Sciences at Paris, and the Academy at Berlin.

The last alone deigned to reply; they told him his discovery was an illusion. Apparently they knew all about it, without investigating. There is no dogmatism so unqualified, no certainty so cocksure, as that of complete ignorance.

The method at first was probably a system of magnetic passes or strokings of the diseased part by the hand of the doctor. But, as the patients increased in number, a more wholesale method had to be devised. Consequently Mesmer invented the famous "*baquet*". This was a large tub, filled with bottles of water previously "magnetised" by Mesmer.

The bottles were arranged to radiate from the centre, some of them with necks pointing away from it and some pointing towards it. They rested on powdered glass and iron filings, and the tub itself was filled with water. In short, it was a sort of glorified travesty of a galvanic battery. From it, long iron rods, jointed and movable, protruded through holes in the lid. These the patients held, or applied to the region of their disease, as they sat in a circle round the *baquet*. Mesmer and his assistants walked about, supplementing the treatment by pointing with the fingers, or with iron rods, at the diseased parts.

All this may seem, at first sight, very absurd. But the fact remains that Mesmer certainly wrought cures. And apparently he frequently succeeded in curing or greatly alleviating, where other doctors had completely failed. It is no longer possible for any instructed person to regard Mesmer as a charlatan who knowingly deluded the public for his own profit. His theories may have been partly mistaken, but his practical results were indubitable.

It is also worth noting that he treated rich and poor alike, charging the latter no fee. He was a man of great tenderness and kindness of heart, devoted to the cause of the sick and suffering; and the accounts of his patients show the unbounded gratitude which they felt towards him, and the respect in which he was held.

The orthodox doctors, of course, felt otherwise. They were envious and jealous of the foreign innovator and his success. And his fame was too great to allow of his being ignored. Consequently the Royal Society of Medicine (Paris) appointed a commission to inquire into the new treatment. The finding, of course, was adverse. The investigators could not deny the cures, but they fell back on the recuperative force of nature (*vis medicatrix naturæ*) and denied that Mesmer's treatment caused the cure.

Obviously, Mesmer, having treated his patients, could not prove that they would not have recovered if he had *not* treated them; so his critics had a strong position. But, on the other hand, neither can an orthodox doctor prove that *his* cures are due to *his* treatment. If it is *vis medicatrix naturæ* in one case, it may be the same in the other.

Modern medicine is more and more coming to this conclusion— is abandoning drugging as it abandoned bleeding and cautery, and is leaving the patient to nature. This is a significant fact.

But there is good reason to believe that Mesmer's treatment was a real factor in his cures, for in many cases the patient had been treated by orthodox methods for years without effect. Perhaps, as the doctors said, it was "only the recuperative force of Nature", but if the doctors could not set that force to work, and Mesmer somehow could, he is just as much entitled to the credit of the cure as if he had done it by bleeding or drugging. However, by one sort of persecution or another, he was driven out of Paris, and more or less discredited. After a visit to England, he retired to Switzerland, where he lived in obscurity until his death in 1815.

The method was kept alive by various disciples, such as the Marquis de Puységur, Dupotet, Deleuze, and many more, but in an amateurish sort of way. The first-named found that in one of his patients he could induce a trance state which showed peculiar features. In trance, the man knew all that he knew when awake, but when awake he knew nothing of what had happened in trance. This second condition thus seemed to be equivalent to an enlargement of personality.

Both in England and France the medical side came to the front again, in the hands of Braid (a Manchester surgeon who first used the term "hypnotism", from Greek *hypnos*, sleep, and whose book *Neurypnology, or the Rationale of Nervous Sleep* was published in 1843), Liébeault, Bernheim, Elliotson, and Esdaile.

Elliotson and Esdaile still believed in a magnetic effluence, but the idea was given up by Braid and the "Nancy school" (the investigators who followed the lines of Liébeault of Nancy), for it was found that patients could be hypnotised without passes or strokings or any manipulation. Braid told his patients to gaze fixedly at a bright object, *e.g.*, his lancet. Liébeault produced sleep by talking soothingly or commandingly filling the patient's mind with the idea of sleep. In some cases it was found that patients could hypnotise themselves by an effort of will (this was confirmed more recently by Dr Wingfield's experiments with athletic undergraduates at Cambridge), and this disposed of the hitherto supposedly necessary "magnetic effluence" from the operator.

The most modern opinion is pretty much the same. Dr Tuckey, who learnt his method from Liébeault himself, and who practised for twenty years in the West End of London, is convinced that the whole thing is suggestion. So is Dr Bramwell, who shares with Dr Tuckey the leading position among hypnotic practitioners in England. The latter, it may be remarked, was the first qualified medical man to write an important book on the subject in English, after Braid.

The tendency now is to give suggestions without attempting to induce actual trance. It is found with many patients that if they will make their minds passive and receptive, listening to the doctor's suggestions in an absent-minded sort of way, those suggestions—that the health shall improve and the specified symptoms disappear—are carried out. The explanation of this is "wrapped in mystery". No one knows exactly how it comes about. But it seems to be somewhat thus:

The complicated happenings within our bodies, such as the chemical phenomena known as digestion and the physical phenomena such as blood circulation and contraction of involuntary muscles, seem to imply intelligence, though that intelligence is not part of the conscious mind, for we do not consciously direct the processes. They go on all the same—for example—when we are asleep. Presumably, then, there is a mental Something in us, which never sleeps, and which runs the organic machinery. If we could get at this Something, and give it instructions, a part of the machinery which is working wrongly might get attended to and put right. Unfortunately, the ordinary consciousness is in the way. We cannot get at the mechanic in the mill, because we have to go through the office, and the managing director keeps us talking.

Well, in hypnotic trance, or even in the preoccupied "absent-minded" state, we get past the managing director—who is asleep or attending to something else—into the mill. We get at the man who really attends to the machinery. We get past the normal consciousness, and can give our orders to the "subconscious" or "subliminal"—which means "below the threshold". In Myers' phrase, suggestion is a "successful appeal to the subliminal self", but exactly how it comes about, and why the patient usually cannot do it for himself but has to have the suggestion administered by a doctor, we do not know.

Of course the word "suggestion" does not really explain anything. It is a word employed to cover our ignorance. Suggestive methods are as empirical as Mesmer's. In each case a successful appeal is made to the recuperative forces of nature, *vis medicatrix naturæ;* but exactly how or why suggestion does it, we know no more—or hardly any more—than we know how and why Mesmer's *baquet* did it. The fact remains, however, that the thing is done. What we lack is only a satisfactory theory.

At one time it was thought that only functional disorders could be relieved. But it is now recognised that the line between functional and organic is an arbitrary one. If we cannot find definite organic change in tissue, we call the ailment functional; but nevertheless some change there must be, though microscopic or unreachable. Consequently even functional disorders are at bottom organic; and, though of course grave lesions produce the gravest disorders, there is no *à priori* impossibility in a hypnotic cure of even the most radical tissue-degeneration.

However, as a matter of practical fact, the "mechanic" has his limitations, like the normal consciousness. He is not omnipotent. Consequently we cannot be sure of being able to stimulate him to the extent of a cure. It depends on his knowledge and power. But he can always do something, if we can get at him. The chief difficulty is that in many people he is inaccessible.

For instance, I have many times submitted myself to the treatment of Dr Tuckey and another medical friend, without effect. I have each time tried my best to help, making my mind as passive as I could; for I was sure that if a suggestible stage could be reached, some troublesome heart symptoms and insomnia could be alleviated. But I was never able to reach a state even approaching hypnosis. I suppose my normal consciousness could not put itself sufficiently to sleep. Being interested in the scientific aspect of the subject, my consciousness watched the process and analysed its own sensations, instead of "letting go" and subsiding out of the way.

As to the proportion of susceptible persons, observers differ. Wetterstrand and Vogt hold that all sane and healthy people are hypnotisable, and Dr Bramwell's results among strong farm labourers at Goole support that view. Patients with nervous ailments are difficult to hypnotise; out of one hundred such cases in his London practice, Dr Bramwell only influenced eighty. This is the percentage of susceptibles found by Drs Tuckey and Bernheim also.

The insane are usually unhypnotisable, probably because of their inability to concentrate their attention. Out of the 80 per cent. of sane susceptibles, only a small proportion go off into hypnotic sleep; ten according to Tuckey, rather more according to the experience of Bramwell, Forel, and Vogt. Most of the susceptible, however, though retaining consciousness, may be deprived of muscular control. For example, if told that they cannot open their eyes, they find that it is so.

The various "stages" of hypnosis shade gradually into each other, and classifications are not much good. Charcot's three stages of lethargy, catalepsy, and somnambulism are now discredited as true stages. In good subjects they are producible at will, and as observed at the Salpêtrière they were almost certainly due to training.

I have no space for the quoting of detailed medical cases, but it is desirable to emphasise the practical facts and to make the subject as concrete as possible to the reader, so I will quote just one, as illustration, from Dr Bramwell's contribution to *Proceedings of the Society for Psychical Research*, vol. xiv, page 99.

"Neurasthenia; suicidal tendencies. Mr D———, aged 34, 1890; barrister. Formerly strong and athletic. Health began to fail in 1877, after typhoid fever. Abandoned work in 1882, and for eight years was a chronic invalid. Anæmic, dyspeptic, sleepless, depressed. Unable to walk a hundred yards without severe suffering. Constant medical treatment, including six months' rest in bed, without benefit. He was hypnotised from June 2 to September 20, 1890. By the end of July all morbid symptoms disappeared, and he amused himself by working on a farm. He can now walk forty miles a day without undue fatigue." Similar cases are now being recorded in the military hospitals. Soldiers make excellent "subjects".

It has been much debated whether a hypnotised person could be made to commit a crime. Probably not; it is difficult to be quite sure, but the evidence is on the negative side. True, a hypnotised subject will put sugar which he has been told is arsenic into his mother's tea, but his inner self probably knows well enough that it is only sugar. On the other hand, it is certain that a hypnotiser may obtain a remarkable amount of control over specially sensitive subjects, particularly by repeated hypnotisations.

I have seen hypnotised subjects who seemed almost perfect automata, obeying orders as mechanically as if they had no will of their own left. Certainly no one, either man or woman, but particularly the latter, should submit himself or herself to hypnotic treatment except by a qualified person in whom full trust can be reposed. And, even then, in the case of a woman patient, it is well for a third person to be present.

But the stories of the novelists, about subjugated wills, hypnotising from a distance, and all the rest of it, are quite without adequate foundation in fact. There is very little evidence in support of hypnosis produced at a distance, and in the one case where it did seem to occur there had been repeated hypnotisations of the ordinary kind, by which a sort of telepathic rapport was perhaps established (Myers' *Human Personality*, vol. i, page 524).

Hypnotism against the will is a myth; except perhaps in here and there a backboneless person who could be influenced any way, without hypnosis or anything of the kind. The Chicago pamphleteer who wants to teach us how to get on in business by developing a "hypnotic eye" is merely after dollars. It is all bunkum.

There is a sense, however, in which hypnotic treatment can be a help in education and in strengthening the character. Backward and lazy children could probably be improved, and I know cases in which sleep-walking and other bad habits have been cured by suggestion. From this it is but a step to dipsomania, which can often be cured. Dr Tuckey reports seventy cures out of two hundred cases.

F. W. H. Myers, to whose genius doctors as well as psychologists owe their first scientific conceptions in this domain, was extremely optimistic here. He held that though we cannot expect to manufacture saints, any more than we can manufacture geniuses, there is nevertheless enough evidence to show that great things could be done.

"If the subject is hypnotisable, and if hypnotic suggestion be applied with sufficient persistency and skill, no depth of previous baseness and foulness need prevent the man or woman whom we charge with 'moral insanity', or stamp as a 'criminal-born', from rising into a state where he or she can work steadily and render services useful to the community" (*Human Personality*, vol. i, page 199). Experiments on hypnotic lines ought certainly to be carried out in our prisons and reformatories. As to the formerly alleged dangers of such experimentation—dangers of hysteria, etc., alleged by the Charcot school which is now seen to have been quite on a wrong tack—they do not exist, if the operator knows his business.

Says Professor Forel: "Liébeault, Bernheim, Wetterstrand, Van Eeden, De Jong, Moll, I myself, and the other followers of the Nancy school, declare categorically that, although we have seen many thousands of hypnotised persons, we have never observed a single case of mental or bodily harm caused by hypnosis, but, on the contrary, have seen many cases of illness relieved or cured by it". Dr Bramwell fully endorses this, saying emphatically that he has "never seen an unpleasant symptom, even of the most trivial nature, follow the skilled induction of hypnosis" (*Proceedings of the Society for Psychical Research*, vol. xii, page 209).

A proof that *intellectual* powers outside the normal consciousness may be tapped by appropriate methods is afforded by the remarkable experiments of Dr Bramwell, on the appreciation of time by somnambules. He ordered a hypnotised subject to carry out, after arousal, some trivial action, such as making a cross on a piece of paper, at the end of a specified period of time, reckoning from the moment of waking. In the waking state, the patient knew nothing of the order; but a subliminal mental stratum knew, and watched the time, making the subject carry out the order when it fell due.

The period varied from a few minutes to several months, and it was stated in various ways, *e.g.* on one occasion Dr Bramwell ordered the action to be carried out in "24 hours and 2880 minutes". The order was given at 3.45 p.m. on December 18, and it was carried out correctly at 3.45 p.m. on December 21. In other experiments, the periods given were 4,417, 8,650, 8,680, 8,700, 10,070, 11,470 minutes.

All were correctly timed by the subliminal stratum, the action being promptly carried out at the due moment. In the waking state the patient was quite incapable—as most of us would be—

of calculating mentally when the periods would elapse. But the hypnotic stratum could do it, and this shows that there are intellectual powers which lie outside the field of the normal consciousness. The argument could be further supported by the feats of "calculating boys", who can sometimes solve the most complicated arithmetical problems, without knowing how they do it. They let the problem sink in, and the answer is shot up presently, like the cooked pudding in the geyser.

But these things are still in their infancy. Psychology is working at the subject, but we do not yet know enough to enable us to venture far in the direction of practical application of hypnotic methods in education. It seems likely, however, that further investigation will yield knowledge which may be of inestimable practical value in the training of minds, as well as in the curing of mental and bodily disease.

CHRISTIAN SCIENCE

It has been said, as a kind of jocular epigram, that the Holy Roman Empire was neither holy nor Roman nor an empire. With similar truth it may be said that Christian Science is neither Christian nor science, in any ordinary sense of those words. Still, perhaps we ought to allow an inventor to christen his own creation, even if the name seems inappropriate or likely to cause misunderstanding; and, Mrs Eddy having invented Christian Science as an organised religion—though, as we shall see, borrowing its main features from an earlier prophet—we may admit her right to give a name to her astonishing production. In order that the personal equation may be allowed for, the present writer begs to affirm that he writes as a sympathetic student though not an adherent.

Mary A. Morse Baker was born on July 16th, 1821, of pious parents, at Bow, New Hampshire. Her father was almost illiterate, rather passionate, a keen hand at a bargain, and a Puritan in religion. All the Bakers were a trifle cranky and eccentric, but some of them possessed ability of sorts, though Mary's father made no great success in life. His daughter made up for him afterwards.

The first fifteen years of Mary Baker's life were passed at the old farm at Bow. The place was lonely, the manner of life primitive, and education not a strong point in the community. Mrs Eddy afterwards claimed to have studied in her girlhood days Hebrew, Greek, Latin, natural philosophy, logic, and moral science! It was, however, maintained by her contemporaries that she was backward and indolent, and that "Smith's *Grammar*, and as far as long division in arithmetic", might be taken as indicating the extent of her scholarship. There is certainly some little discrepancy here, and perhaps Mrs Eddy's memory was a trifle at fault. She made no claim to any acquaintance with this formidable array of subjects in the later part of her life, and it seems probable that her contemporaries were right. Her physical beauty, coupled with delicate health, seem to have resulted in "spoiling", for even as a child she dominated her surroundings to a surprising extent.

In 1843 she married George Glover, who died in June, 1844, leaving her penniless. Her only child was born in the September following. After ten years of widowhood she married Daniel Paterson, a travelling dentist. In 1866 they separated, he making some provision for her. In 1873 she obtained a divorce on the ground of desertion. In 1877 she married Asa Gilbert Eddy, who died in 1882.

So much for her matrimonial experiences, which may now be dismissed, as they had no particular influence on her character and career. To prevent confusion, we will call her throughout by the name which is most familiar to us and to the world.

The chief event of Mrs Eddy's remarkable life, the event which put her on the road to fame and fortune, occurred in 1862. This was her meeting with the famous "healer", Phineas Parkhurst Quimby. This latter was an unschooled but earnest and benevolent man, who had made experiments in mesmerism, etc., and who had found—or thought he had found—that people could be cured of their ailments by "faith". He therefore began to work out a system of "mind-cure", which he embodied in voluminous MSS. Patients came to him from far and near, and he treated all, whether they could pay or not. Quimby was much above the level of the common quack, and his character commands our respect. He was a man of great natural intelligence, and was admirable in all his dealings with family, friends, and patients.

Mrs Eddy visited him at Portland in 1862, her aim being treatment for her continued ill-health. She claims to have been cured—in three weeks—though it is clear from her later letters that the cure was not complete. Still, great improvement was apparently effected, for she had been almost bedridden, with some kind of spinal or hysterical complaint, for eight years previously. But Quimby's effect on her was greater mentally even than physically. She became interested in his system, watched his treatment of patients, borrowed his MSS., and mastered his teachings. In 1864 she visited him again, staying two or three months, and prosecuting her studies. She now seemed to have formed a definite desire to assist in teaching his system. No doubt she dimly saw a possible career opening out in front of her; though we need not attribute her desire entirely to mere ambition or greed, for it is probable that Quimby did a great amount of genuine good, and his pupil would naturally imbibe some of his zeal for the relief of suffering humanity.

In 1866 Quimby died, aged sixty-four. His pupil decided to put on the mantle of her teacher, but more as propagandist and religious prophet than as healer. In this latter capacity perhaps her sex was against her. (Even now the average individual seems to have a sad lack of confidence in the "lady doctor"!) But she was poor, and prospects did not seem promising. For some time she drifted about among friends—chiefly spiritualists—preparing MSS. and teaching Quimbyism to anyone who would listen. (She afterwards denied her indebtedness to Quimby, claiming direct revelation. "No human pen nor tongue taught me the science contained in this book, *Science and Health*, and neither tongue nor pen can overthrow it."—*Science and Health*, p. 110, 1907 edition.)

Though unsuccessful as healer (in spite of her later claim to have healed Whittier of "incipient pulmonary consumption" in one visit), she certainly had the knack of teaching—had the power of inspiring enthusiasm and of inoculating others with her ideas. In 1870 she turned up at Lynn, Mass., with a pupil named Richard Kennedy, a lad of twenty-one. Her aim being to found a religious organisation based on practical results (the prayer of faith shall heal the sick, etc.), it was necessary to work with a pupil-practitioner. Accordingly she and Kennedy took offices at Lynn, and "Dr Kennedy" appeared on a signboard affixed to a tree.

Immediate success followed. Patients crowded the waiting-rooms. Kennedy did the "healing" and Mrs Eddy organised classes, which were recruited from the ranks of patients and friends; fees, a hundred dollars for twelve lessons, afterwards raised to three hundred dollars for seven lessons. Before long, however, she quarrelled with Kennedy, and in 1872 they separated, but not before she had reaped about six thousand dollars as her share of the harvest. It was her first taste of success, after weary years of toil and stress and hysteria and eccentricity. Naturally, like Alexander, she sighed for further conquest. *L'appétit vient en mangeant.* And, though in her fiftieth year, she was now more energetic than ever.

Her next move was the purchase of a house at 8, Broad Street, Lynn, which became the first official headquarters of Christian Science. In 1875 appeared her famous book, *Science and Health, With Key to the Scriptures*, which was financed by two of its author's friends. The first edition was of a thousand copies. As it sold but slowly, she persuaded her chief practitioner, Daniel Spofford, to give up his practice and to devote himself to advertising the book and pushing its sale. Since then it has been revised many times, and the editions are legion. Loyal disciples of the better-educated sort have assisted in its rewriting, and it is now a very presentable kind of affair as to its literary form. Most, if not all, of the editions have been sold at a minimum of $3.18 per copy, with *editions de luxe* at $5 or more, and the author's other works are published at similarly high prices. All Christian Scientists were commanded to buy the works of the Reverend Mother, and all successive editions of those works. It is not surprising that Mrs Eddy should leave a fortune of a million and a half dollars. It may be mentioned here that she moved from Lynn to Boston in 1882, thence to Concord (New Hampshire) in 1889, and finally to a large mansion in a Boston suburb which she bought for $100,000, spending a similar sum in remodelling and enlarging. The modern prophet does not dwell in the wilderness, subsisting on locusts and wild honey. He—or she—has moved with the times, and has a proper respect for the almighty dollar and the comforts of civilisation.

In 1881 was founded the Massachusetts Metaphysical College. This imposingly-named institution never had any special buildings, and its instructions were mostly given in Mrs Eddy's parlour, Mrs Eddy herself constituting all the faculty. Four thousand students passed through the "College" in seven years, at the end of which period it ceased to exist. The fees were usually $300 for seven lessons, as before. Few gold-mines pay as well as did the "Metaphysical College". The fact does not at first sight increase our respect for the alleged cuteness of the inhabitants of the States. But, on further investigation, the murder is out. Most of these students probably earned back by "healing" much more than they paid Mrs Eddy. Our respect for Uncle Sam's business shrewdness returns in full force.

The experiment of conducting religious services had been made by Mrs Eddy at Lynn in 1875, but the first Christian Science Church was not chartered until 1879. The Scientists met, however, in various public halls of Boston, until 1894, when a church was built. This was soon outgrown, and 10,000 of the faithful pledged themselves to raise two million dollars for its enlargement. The new building was finished in 1906. Its auditorium holds five thousand people. The walls are decorated with texts signed "Jesus, the Christ," and "Mary Baker G. Eddy"—these names standing side by side.

The following examples, culled almost at random, will further show how great is her conviction that she has the Truth, how vigorously she bulls her own stocks (somehow, financial metaphors seem inevitable when writing of Mrs Eddy):

"God has been graciously fitting me during many years for the reception of this final revelation of the absolute divine Principle of scientific mental healing". (*Science and Health*, p. 107.)

"I won my way to absolute conclusion through divine revelation, reason and demonstration". (*Ibid.*, p. 109.)

"To those natural Christian Scientists, the ancient worthies, and to Christ Jesus, God certainly revealed the Spirit of Christian Science, if not the absolute letter". (*Ibid.*, p. 483.)

"The theology of Christian Science is truth; opposed to which is the error of sickness, sin, and death, that truth destroys". (*Miscellaneous Writings*, p. 62.)

"Christian Science is the unfolding of true Metaphysics, that is, of Mind, or God, and His attributes. Science rests on principle and demonstration. The Principle of Christian Science is divine". (*Ibid.*, p. 69.)

The following maybe quoted as an example of mixed good and evil, with a certain flavour of unconscious humour:

"Hate no one; for hatred is a plague-spot that spreads its virus and kills at last. If indulged, it masters us; brings suffering to its possessor throughout time, and beyond the grave. If you have been badly wronged, forgive and forget: God will recompense this wrong, and punish, more severely than you could, him who has striven to injure you". (*Miscellaneous Writings*, p. 12.)

The advice is good, but it is not new. And Mrs Eddy seemed to experience a special joy in the thought that by leaving our enemies alone they will receive from God a more effective trouncing than we with our poor appliances could administer. The ideal Christian would not want his enemies handed over to the inquisitor—he would beg for them to be let off. "Father, forgive them, for they know not what they do!" That is the Christian attitude. It is perhaps too high for ordinary mortals to attain to, but Mrs Eddy made such high claims that we are entitled to judge her by correspondingly high standards.

The form of service in the various Christian Science churches at first included a sermon. But Mrs Eddy soon saw that this might introduce discord: for the preachers might differ in their interpretations of *Science and Health*. And Mrs Eddy above all things aimed at unity in order to keep the control in her own hands. Therefore, in 1895, she forbade preaching altogether. The Bible and *Science and Health, With Key to the Scriptures*, were to be read from, but no explanatory comments were to be made. The services comprise Sunday morning and evening readings from these two books, with music; the Wednesday evening experience meeting; and the communion service, once or twice a year only. There is no baptismal, marriage, or burial service, and weddings and funerals are never conducted in Christian Science churches.

As to church government, there was a nominal board of directors, but Mrs Eddy had supreme power. She could appoint or dismiss at will. The Church was hers, body and soul. Probably no other religious leader ever had such an unqualified sway. The Holy Father at Rome is a mere figurehead in comparison with the late Reverend Mother.

In June, 1907, there were in all 710 branch churches. Of these, twenty-five were in Canada, fourteen in Britain, two in Ireland, four in Australia, one in South Africa, eight in Mexico, two in Germany, one in Holland, one in France, and the remainder in the States. There were also 295 societies not yet incorporated into churches. The total membership of the 710 churches was probably about 50,000. (In *Pulpit and Press*, p. 82, Mrs Eddy puts the number at 100,000 to 200,000; and this was in 1895. Some claim that the total number of adherents is as high as a million. But these are probably exaggerated estimates.) About one-tenth of these make their living by their faith. Here we come to the secret of Christian Science success.

There are about 400 authorised Christian Science "healers", and many who practise without diploma but not without pay. These people treat sick folks, receiving fees. Their method is to assure the patient that he is under a delusion in thinking himself ill, that matter is an illusion, that God is All, etc. It sounds very absurd. But the curious thing is that many people have been cured by this treatment, and—naturally—these people become ardent Christian Scientists. It is by the practical application that Christian Science as a religion lives and thrives. As to the kind of diseases cured, the most extravagant claims are made. In *Miscellaneous Writings*, p. 41, Mrs Eddy definitely states that "all classes of disease" can be healed by her method. After careful sifting of much evidence, however, Dr Myers and his brother (F. W. H. Myers) found that no proof was forthcoming for the cure of definite organic disease by Christian Science methods. (*Proceedings of the Society for Psychical Research*, vol. ix, p. 160; also *Journal*, vol. viii, p. 247.) Undoubtedly they have been, and are continually, efficient in relieving, and even curing, many functional disorders which have resisted ordinary medical treatment—and it must be remembered that many functional derangements are as serious, subjectively, as grave organic disease—and consequently it is undeniable that Christian Science often does good. But it is probable that the same amount of good, and perhaps more, could be done by the hypnotic or suggestive treatment of a qualified medical man, or perhaps by other forms of "faith-healing". The Christian Scientist is using suggestion; but he couples it up with religion, and thus, perhaps—with some people—succeeds in driving the suggestion home with greater force. It is noteworthy that similar attempts are now being made in other directions—witness the Emmanuel movement in New York, the Faithists and various "psycho-therapeutic" societies in England, and the tendency in some quarters (Bishop of London) to return to anointing and laying on of hands by clergymen.

Psychologically, Mrs Eddy is at least classified, if not entirely explained, by one word—monoideism. She was a person of one idea. These people, for whom we usually have the simpler term of "crank", are common enough. I have no personal acquaintance with the circle-squaring and perpetual-motion cranks mentioned by De Morgan (*The Budget of Paradoxes*), but I know a "flat-earth" crank, and am well acquainted with a "British-Israelite" crank, who seems to derive unspeakable joy—tempered only by his failure to convert me—from the thought that we Britishers are veritably the descendants of one or more of the Lost Tribes. All these people are conscious of a mission. They have had a revelation, and are anxious to impart it. Their efforts may not be due to the "last infirmity of noble mind", still less to a lower motive. They may just be built that way. The majority of them, like my Lost-Tribes friend, get no hearing because of the inflexible pragmatism of a stiffnecked and utilitarian generation. "What difference does it make whether we are the Tribes or not?" asks the man in the street. And he passes on with a shrug or a grin, according to temperament. This terrible pragmatic test makes short work of many amiable cranks. And it is just here that Christian Science scores its point; for it cures physical disease, thereby becoming intensely practical. Health is the chief "good" of life. Anything that will restore it to an ailing body commands immediate and universal respect. Christian Science therefore appeals, on its practical side, to the deepest thing in us—to the primal instinct of self-preservation. Hence its success.

It is possible to blame Mrs Eddy unjustly for her love of power as such. She was not unique in this respect. The difference is that Mrs Eddy succeeded while the others have not, and are consequently not heard of. My Lost-Tribes friend would be as autocratic as anybody if he had the chance; but his motive would not be greed of power, but rather the overmastering desire to push his cause, to proselytise, to promulgate his one idea, almost by force, if such a thing were possible. Most of us know a few fanatics of this kind. The objects of their devotion are varied—

one is mad north-north-west, another south-south-east—but all suffer from a lack of balance, a lack of proper distribution of interest. Of course, we may cheerfully admit that we are all more or less specialists in our several departments, and that the line between sanity and insanity is rather arbitrary. We all seem more or less mad to those who do not agree with us.

The good and true part of Christian Science is its demonstration of the influence of mind on body, and of the usefulness of inducing mental states of an optimistic character. It may, of course, be said that we need no Mrs Eddy to tell us this. True, we don't. The great seers and poets have always taught optimism, and the influence of mind on body was medically recognised—more or less—long before even Quimby's time. But we must remember that different minds need different treatment—need their nutriment and stimulant in different forms, to suit the various mental digestions and receptive powers. Consequently, though we may prefer Browning for optimism and the doctors for hypnotic therapeutics, we need not complain if others prefer Mrs Eddy and her disciples. If they get good from their way of putting things, and if that good manifests itself in their character and life—in their total reaction on the world—by all means let them continue to walk in their chosen way. It would be wrong to try to turn them. The system "works"; therefore it is true for them. The tree is known by its fruits. And the fruits of Christian Science are undoubtedly often good. In this complex world nothing is unmixedly good, and harm is no doubt done occasionally. But, on the whole, it seems probable that Mrs Eddy, with all her hysteria and morbidities and rancours and queerness, has been a power for good in the world. Her writings meet a want which some people feel, or, rather, provide them with a useful impulse in the direction of physical and spiritual regeneration. If you can make a sick person stop brooding over his ailments and worrying over things in general, you have achieved something which enormously increases his chance of recovery; and if you can make him turn all his thoughts and energies in the direction of recovery, and all his emotional powers in the direction of love and goodwill to his fellow-men and towards God, there is no limit to the powers which may be put in operation. In spite of all our achievements in science—and they have been great—we are only, as Newton said, picking up pebbles on the sea-shore. Nature is boundless; we can fix no limits to her powers. And we know so little, really, about disease, that I am not at all prepared to deny the Christian Science claims, even with regard to organic disease. The distinction between organic and functional is in our own inabilities, not in the nature of the case; we call a disease "organic" when we find definite tissue-change, and "functional" when we do not; but in the latter case there must be some organic basis, though too small perhaps to be discoverable—say a lesion in a tiny nerve. Consequently I regard the question of Christian Science cures as entirely one of evidence. I keep an open mind. If I come across enough evidence, I will believe that it can cure tuberculosis of the lungs and other diseases, as claimed, whether I can understand how it does it or not. At present, like Dr Myers, I am not convinced; but I have seen enough of Christian Science results among my own friends to prevent me from denying anything. I merely suspend judgment. But I do believe that the power of the mind over the body is so great that almost anything is possible; and I think that the medical advance of the next half-century will be chiefly in this hitherto neglected direction. I happen to know that this, or something very near this, was the strongly-held opinion of the late Professor William James of Harvard, who, in addition to being the most brilliant psychologist of his generation, was also a qualified doctor of medicine.

JOAN OF ARC

Great results often flow from small causes. Pascal said that if Cleopatra's nose had been shorter the history of the world would have been different. Similarly it may be truly said that if a peasant girl of Domrémy had not had hallucinations, France would now have been a British province. And it is curious to reflect that the Church which burnt her as a heretic and sorcerer has her, and her only, to thank for such hold as it still maintains on France, for the latter would have become Protestant if England had won. The Roman church now recognises this, and has beatified the Maid. The next step will be her canonisation as a saint. Thus does the whirligig of Time bring its revenges.

Jeanne d'Arc was born in the village of Domrémy near Vaucouleurs, on the border of Champagne and Lorraine, on January 6th, 1412. She was taught to spin and to sew, but not to read or write, these accomplishments being beyond what was necessary for people in her station of life. Her parents were devout, and she was brought up piously. Her nature was gentle, modest, and religious, but with no physical weakness or morbid abnormality—on the contrary, she was exceptionally strong, as her later history proves.

At or about the age of thirteen, Jeanne began to experience what psychology now calls "auditory hallucinations". That is, she heard voices—usually accompanied by a bright light—when no visible person was present. This, of course, is a common symptom of impending mental disorder; but no insanity developed in Jeanne d'Arc. Startled she naturally was at first, but continuation led to familiarity and trust. The voices gave good counsel of a commonplace kind, as, for instance, that she "must be a good girl and go regularly to church." Soon, however, she began to have visions: saw St Michael, St Catherine, and St Margaret; was given instructions as to her mission; eventually made her way to the Dauphin; put herself at the head of 6,000 men, and advanced to the relief of Orleans, which was besieged by the conquering English. After a fortnight of hard fighting the siege was raised, and the enemy driven off. The tide of war had turned, and in three months the Dauphin was crowned King at Rheims, as Charles the Seventh.

At this point Jeanne felt that her mission was accomplished. But her wish to return to her family was over-ruled by king and archbishop, and she took part in the further fighting against the allied English and Burgundian forces, showing great bravery and tactical skill. But in November, 1430, in a desperate sally from Compiegne—which was besieged by the Duke of Burgundy—she fell into the enemy's hands, was sold to the English, and thrown into a dungeon at their headquarters in Rouen.

After a year's imprisonment she was brought to trial—a mock trial before the Bishop of Beauvais, in an ecclesiastical court. Learned doctors of the church did their best to entangle the simple girl in their dialectical toils; but she showed a remarkable power of keeping to her simple affirmations and of avoiding heretical statements. "God has always been my Lord in all that I have done". But the trial was only pretence, for her fate was already decided. She was burnt to death, amid the jeers and execration of a rabble of brutal soldiery, in a Rouen market-place on May 30th, 1431.

The life of the Maid supplies a problem which orthodox science cannot solve. She was a simple peasant girl, with no ambitions hankering after a career. She rebelled pathetically against her mission. "I had far rather rest and spin by my mother's side, for this is no work of my choosing, but I must go and do it, for my Lord wills it." She cannot be dismissed on the "simple idiot" theory of Voltaire, for her genius in war and her aptitude in repartee undoubtedly prove exceptional mental powers, unschooled though she was in what we call education. We cannot call her a mere hysteric, for her health and strength were superb.

A man of science once said to an Abbé: "Come to the Salpêtrière Hospital, and I will show you twenty Jeannes d'Arc." To which the Abbé responded: "Has one of them given us back Alsace and Lorraine?"

There is the crux, as Andrew Lang quietly remarked.

The retort was certainly neat. Still, though the Salpêtrière hysterics have not won back Alsace and Lorraine, it is nevertheless true that a great movement may be started, or kept going when started, by fraud, hallucination, and credulity. The Mormons, for example, are a strong body, but the origins of their faith will not bear much criticism. *The Book of Mormon*, handed down from heaven by an angel, is more than we can swallow. No one saw its "metal leaves"—from which Joseph Smith translated—except Joseph himself. We have our own opinion about Joseph's truthfulness. Somewhat similarly with spiritualism. The great movement is there, based partly on fact as I believe, but supported by some fraud and much ignorance and credulity. May it not have been somewhat thus with Jeanne? She delivered France, and her importance in history is great; but may not her mission and her doings have been the outcome of merely subjective hallucinations, induced by the brooding of her specially religious and patriotic mind on the woes of her country? The army, being ignorant and superstitious, would readily believe in the supernatural character of her mission, and great energy and valour would follow as a matter of course—for a man fights well when he believes that Providence is on his side.

That is the usual kind of theory in explanation of the facts. But it is not fully satisfactory. How came it—one may ask—that this untutored peasant girl could persuade not only the rude soldiery, but also the Dauphin and the court, of her Divine appointment? How came she to be given the command of an army? Surely a post of such responsibility and power would not be given to a peasant girl of eighteen, on the mere strength of her own claim to inspiration. It seems, at least, very improbable.

Now it seems (though the materialistic school of historians conveniently ignore or belittle it) that there is strong evidence in support of the idea that Jeanne gave the Dauphin some proof of the possession of supernormal faculties. In fact, the evidence is so strong that Mr Lang called it "unimpeachable"—and Mr Lang did not usually err on the side of credulity in these matters. Among other curious things, Jeanne seems to have repeated to Charles the words of a prayer which he had made mentally, and she also made some kind of clairvoyant discovery of a sword hidden behind the altar of Fierbois church. Schiller's magnificent dramatic poem *"Die Jungfrau von Orleans,"* though unhistorical in some details, is substantially accurate on these points concerning clairvoyance and mind-reading.

As to the voices and visions, a Protestant will have a certain prejudice with regard to the St Michael, St Catherine, and St Margaret stories, though he may very possibly be wrong in his disbelief. But, waiving that, it may be true that some genuine inspiration was truly given to the Maid from the deeper strata of her own soul, and that these monitions externalised themselves in the forms in which her thought habitually ran. If she had been a Greek of two thousand years earlier, her visions would probably have taken the form of Apollo and Pallas Athene; yet they might equally well have contained truth and good counsel, as did the utterances of the Oracles.

And, speaking of the Greeks, we may remember that the wisest of that race had similar experiences. Socrates—the pre-eminent type of sanity and mental burliness—was counselled by his "daimon"; by a warning Voice which, truly, did not give positive advice like Jeanne's, but which intervened to stop him when about to make some wrong decision. Again—to jump suddenly down to modern times—Charles Dickens says in his letters that the characters of his novels took on a kind of independent existence, and that Mrs Gamp, his greatest creation, spoke to him (generally in church) as with an actual voice. In fact, all cases of creative genius, whether in literature, art, or invention, are examples of an uprush from unknown mental depths: the process is not the same as the intellectual process of reasoning. In these cases, as for instance with Socrates, Jeanne d'Arc, Dickens, the deeper strata of the mind may be supposed to send up thoughts so vigorously that they become externalised as hallucinations; not necessarily morbid or injurious, though of course many hallucinations are undoubtedly both. The inspiration rises from below the conscious threshold. It is as if "given"; and the normal conscious mind looks on in passive astonishment. *Alles ist als wie geschenkt,* says Goethe—and he knew, if anybody did. A similar thing happens, on a more ordinary plane, when a problem that has baffled the working mind is solved in sleep. In short, the normal consciousness is not all there is of us; there are levels and powers below the threshold. And it seems likely that the new psychology is on the track of a better explanation of Socrates and Jeanne d'Arc, as well as of the nature of genius in general, than has yet been excogitated by the philosophers. Certainly these things supply interesting material for study, and many curious discoveries are now being made in this field of research.

IS THE EARTH ALIVE?

Some of the ancients thought the earth was an animal. It has its hard and soft parts, its bone and flesh—rock and soil—as the Norse cosmology pictured it; also its blood, of seas, rivers, and the like. To a coast-dwelling people, the rhythmic inflow and outflow of the tides would suggest a huge slow blood-pulsation, or a breathing. And heat increases with depth, in mine or cave; fire spouts from Etna and Vesuvius; evidently the earth is hotter inside than at the surface, as animals are hotter inside than on their skins. Some such animal-notion was held by Plato, and by some of the later Stoics; though it does not seem to have been worked out in detail. And the Greek, Indian, or Egyptian theology which made the earth a goddess and the bride of Heaven or the sun, is still more indefinite, or is crudely anthropomorphic and primitive.

Modern approximations have been chiefly in poetry, and are pan-psychic rather than animistic; as in Pope's *Essay on Man:*

All are but parts of one stupendous whole, Whose body Nature is, and God the soul,

and in Wordsworth's *Tintern Abbey* where the presence which disturbs him with the joy of elevated thoughts is felt to be the Spirit which has its dwelling in the light of setting suns and the round ocean and the living air:

A motion and a spirit that impels All thinking things, all objects of all thought, And rolls through all things. Therefore am I still A lover of the meadows and the woods, And mountains; and all that we behold From this green earth; of all the mighty world Of eye, and ear.

Emerson expresses the same thought in *Pan* and in much of his prose—*Nature, The Over Soul, Self-Reliance.* William James, in early days before his pluralistic development, thought that an *anima mundi* thinking in all of us was a more likely hypothesis than that of "a lot of individual souls"; and Leibnitz, among other metaphysical great ones, Spinozistically speaks of "un seul esprit qui est universel et qui anime tout l'univers". Finally, to quote a modern of the moderns, we find Mr H. G. Wells finely saying that "between you and me as we set our minds together, and between us and the rest of mankind, there is *something*, something real, something that rises through us and is neither you nor me, that comprehends us, that is thinking here and using me and you to play against each other in that thinking just as my finger and thumb play against each other as I hold this pen with which I write". (*First and Last Things*, p. 67.)

But these various poets and thinkers, while suggesting a soul-side of the material universe, have not ventured to attribute spirits to specific lumps of matter such as the planets. Science has banished those celestial genii. Kepler and Newton substituted for them the "bald and barren doctrine of gravitation", to the disgust of the theologically orthodox. It is possible, however, that science did not banish these planetary spirits, but only prevented us from seeing them, by turning our eyes in another direction, towards the laws according to which the material universe works; as if we should become so absorbed in the chemistry and physics of blood oxidation, digestion, cerebral change, and the like, as to forget that the human body has a consciousness associated with it. It may be that we are too materialistic in our astronomy. Perhaps Lorenzo was right, even about the music of the spheres; and that our deafness, not their silence, is the reason why we do not hear it.

The nineteenth century produced a thinker who revived the animistic idea in an improved form. He elaborated it into a system of philosophy, welding into it the discoveries of science, and leaving room for any further advance in that direction. At the same time he showed that his system was essentially religious, and indeed quite consistent with Christianity in its best interpretations. But his writings fell almost dead from the press, for he was before his time. The scientific men were materialists, and sneered at a system which recognised a spiritual world; while the orthodox Christians were scared by its evolutionary method and its acceptance of Darwinism when the latter arrived—for the philosophy preceded it—and also by the novelty of some of its ideas.

Gustav Theodor Fechner was born on April 19, 1801, at Gross-Särchen in what is now Silesia, then under the Elector of Saxony. He studied at Leipzig, and was appointed professor of Physics at the University there, in 1834. He conducted several scientific journals, wrote text-books, translated Biot's *Physics* (4 vols.) Thénard's *Chemistry* (6 vols.) and a work on cerebral pathology; also edited an eight-volume *Encyclopædia* of which he wrote about a third himself, lectured, and made researches in electro-magnetism which injured his eyesight. His chief scientific work, *Elements of Psycho-Physics*, was published in 1859, additions being made in 1877 and 1882. "Fechner's Law", the fundamental law of psychophysics (that sensation varies in the ratio of the logarithm of impression) is now an internationally current term. Men like Paulsen and Wundt do not hesitate to call Fechner master. His chief philosophical work is *Zend-Avesta* (3 vols.) published in 1851, and rearranged and condensed in *Die Tagesansicht gegenüber der Nachtansicht* (1879); but he published also many subsidiary volumes. Only one of his works has appeared in English—the small volume on *Life After Death*—and even this had to be brought out by an American publisher! Yet Fechner is, as Professor William James said, "a philosopher in the great sense ... little known as yet to English readers, but destined, I am persuaded, to wield more and more influence as time goes on". (*A Pluralistic Universe*, pp. 135, 149.) The prophecy is already beginning to come true.

Fechner always begins with the known and indisputable, arguing thence to the unknown. His method is thus analogical and scientific. It is the only method that a scientific generation will tolerate. Its results may be disputed, but so can the results of science. Even mathematics gives us no certainties, for something must always be taken for granted. In philosophising by analogy, we do at least keep in close touch with experience; we do not evaporate the world into an "unearthly ballet of bloodless categories". And if the analogies point mostly one way, with only weak ones pointing the other, the result may be at least acceptable as a working hypothesis, even if not "demonstrable".

Man is a living, thinking, feeling being. He is on the surface of a nearly spherical body, which he calls the earth, out of which his material part has arisen. The elements of his body are the same as those in the earth. His carbon, nitrogen, oxygen, and hydrogen are the carbon, nitrogen, oxygen, and hydrogen of the coal measures, soils, atmosphere, oceans, of the earth. The calcium carbonate of his bones is the calcium carbonate of her rocks as seen in cliffs at Flamborough and Dover. He is bone of her bone, flesh of her flesh. Sometimes he calls her Mother Earth, and involuntarily speaks the truth in jest. In Siberia the Tartar word for the earth is "Mamma"—a curious fact. Indeed, the bond between the earth and her children is much closer than in the case of a human mother and her child; for we remain, all our lives, actually *part* of the planet's mass. If our bodies were suddenly annihilated, the earth's gravitative attraction would be altered, and the whole solar system would have to readjust itself to the slight diminution. We belong to the earth. We are a film of cells on her skin. In Piccadilly and the Bowery (and Throgmorton and Wall Streets?) we are—alas!—an eczematous patch.

But here it may be objected that man is more than a mere body. Quite true. Man has experiences of an order different from the material one. You cannot express joy and sorrow by chemical equations or number of foot-pounds. Even if there is a material

89

equivalent or necessary concomitant, of electrical or chemical change in cerebral tissue or what not, the fact of the non-material experience remains a reality. To indicate this side of human life, we call it the spiritual side. We say that man is matter and spirit, body and soul. This is quite justifiable and right, whether we can define the terms or not. Definition means explaining a word by means of others that are better known. And as we cannot get any closer to reality than our own experience, which *is* reality to us, and as the two words conveniently classify two great departments of experience, we justifiably say that we are soul and body. Very well; the body, then, when we die, returns to the earth, from which indeed it has not been severed, except as being a point at which a special kind of activity was manifested. What then of the soul? Shall it not return to the earth-soul, as the body returns to the earth-body?

Man has arisen out of the earth. And can the dead give birth to the living? Such an idea is self-contradictory. If the Earth has produced us, it cannot be really a mere dead lump, as nineteenth-century materialistic science regarded it. It must be alive. The fifteen hundred millions or so of human beings who live on its surface like microscopic insects on the body of an elephant, or like epidermis-cells on our own bodies, constitute in their total weight and size only an almost infinitesimal proportion of the earth's mass. The earth is 8,000 miles in diameter; if human beings were so numerous that they could only stand up, wedged together all over its surface, tropics and poles, land and water—the latter covers seven-tenths of it—they would only be like a skin $1/200,000$th part of an inch thick, on a globe a yard in diameter. The total mass of all the living creatures on the earth's surface, including all animals and all vegetation, is almost inconceivably small, as compared with the mass of the earth. Is it not a trifle ludicrous to find some of these little creatures looking down so condescendingly on the remainder of the planet? Emerson was among the few who have seen the joke, for in

Hamatreya he satirises those who boast of possessing pieces of the earth:

Where are these men? Asleep beneath their grounds: And strangers, fond as they, their furrows plough. Earth laughs in flowers, to see her boastful boys Earth-proud, proud of the earth which is not theirs; Who steer the plough, but cannot steer their feet Clear of the grave.

And the earth sings:

They called me theirs, Who so controlled me; Yet every one Wished to stay, and is gone, How am I theirs, If they cannot hold me, But I hold them?

A very natural objection to the idea of the earth being full of life and mind—as my body is full of my life and my mind—is that the inorganic part of the planet presents no evidence of such. It does not act as if it were alive and conscious. But this begs the whole question. If you decide beforehand that all evidence for the existence of mind must be the sort of phenomena exhibited by the things we call living, the business is settled, and it is clear that the inorganic kingdom is without consciousness. There is then no sign of mind anywhere except in that infinitesimally thin and indeed discontinuous skin which is made up of living individuals on the earth's surface. But is it not somewhat presumptuous to dogmatise thus? Why should mind always manifest itself in the same way? Non-living matter does not show vital activities, but it does show other activities, quite systematic and non-chaotic and comprehensible ones. How could "dead" matter have any activity at all? Even Haeckel postulates a sort of mind in the atom, and we have heard of "mind-stuff" before, from an equally determined materialist. Indeed, how can we rationalise the behaviour of phosphorus in oxygen but by saying that the two elements like each other so well that they rush to combine whenever possible? If carbon has great "affinity," showing a tendency to combine with many atoms of other elements in various complicated ways—at least as regards its favourite types—it is reasonable to regard it as a much-loving element—the polygamous Solomon of the elements. If fluorine will have nothing to do with other substances—except under protest, when persuaded by Miss Hydrogen, whose gaiety and levity sometimes overcome its sulkiness, bringing it also into the society of calcium and one or two other metals—we must say that fluorine is unsociable, morbidly self-centred, or perhaps mystically disposed, like Thoreau, happy by his pond, alone. Chemical affinity is the loves of the elements.

Rising to the next grade of complexity above atoms, we find that molecular movements, visible in the apparently representative Brownian movements of particles, recall the fidget of a bunch of midges, and thereby suggest a sort of life. They disobey the second law of thermodynamics, rising in a lighter liquid, as midges rise in the tenuous air. Of course no one can deny that in the things we call living there are phenomena not seen elsewhere, and some of these are quite probably not understandable at all, in terms of measurement or imagery, as we can understand the Brownian movements by irregular bombardment of molecules. We cannot understand the relation between a supposed brain-change and the corresponding mental fact. The two orders of being seem disjunctive. Perhaps these things are too close to us to be understood; perhaps we cannot understand life and consciousness because we are ourselves alive and conscious—as we cannot lift ourselves by pulling at our boot tops, and cannot see our own faces because the eyes that see are *in* the face that is to be seen. Still the distinction between life at its lowest and non-life at its highest (crystals?) is so small that we may yet effect a smooth transition—may somehow see a continuity which now eludes us. And it seems likely that this will be effected by an extension of the mind-idea down into the inorganic, rather than by any explanation of life by physical and chemical concepts.

Again, on the larger scale, may not cohesion, as well as chemical affinity, be a sort of affection; in this case a kind of wide social friendship—the "adhesive love" of Whitman, which is to supersede "amative love"—as against the fierce and narrow loves of the elements? A. C. Benson in *Joyous Gard* (p. 128) quotes a geologist who says:

It is not by any means certain that stones do not have a certain obscure life of their own; I have sometimes thought that their marvellous cohesion may be a sign of life, and that if life were withdrawn, a mountain might in a moment become a heap of sliding sand.

Yes, and even in sand-grains there is cohesion of particles, and in the smallest particles huge numbers of molecules, and again—still smaller—atoms and electrons. Something elusive yet tremendously potent is still there, in the sand. It would be rash to call it dead and mindless. There seems more sense in admitting that there is something akin to what we know as life and mind in ourselves, permeating the material universe.

And if—to come back to our own planet—if the earth is a living organism, there will naturally be distribution of function, as there is in our own bodies. It would be absurd for the eye to deny life and perception to ear or skin just because their mode of activity is different. It is wiser to concede life and mind where-ever there is action. In the present state of affairs, not only do we get into difficulties by our rash assumption that there is no mind without protoplasm (*ohne Phosphor kein Gedanke*, as the old materialist too boldly said), but we find it impossible to draw the line between living and non-living. Drops of oil exhibit amœboid movements, and at the lower end of life the slime-mass becomes so undifferentiated as to be very much in a borderland between the two states. Probably non-living substances gradate into living ones by imperceptible *differentiæ*, as man would be found to gradate back into an anthropoid ape or something of the kind if we could see all the stages. Nature does not make jumps. Where she seems to do so, it is only because we cannot see how she gets from one place to another distant one. But when we scrutinise the interspace, we see that there is a path. Nature does not jump. She glides.

It is on this line of thought that the disagreement between the schools represented by Sir Edward Schäfer and Dr Hans Driesch respectively may, perhaps, be happily resolved. No doubt each may have to make concessions. The mechanist must not claim that mind is *only* an affair of nitrogenous colloids, for this would be a large assumption built on a very small foundation; no biologist, however much he knows about nitrogenous colloids, can in any conceivable sense explain his joy in a sunset or a symphony by reference to those substances. Physical causes have physical effects; to say that they cause anything non-physical (*i.e.* mental) is really talking nonsense. And, on the other hand, the vitalist must not deny consciousness to non-protoplasmic Nature. Negations are dangerous. It is extremely risky to say that a Matterhorn has less spiritual significance—in itself and for the whole, and not only for us—than a cretin who wanders useless and unbeautiful about its lower slopes. The activities of the two are different, that is all we are justified in saying. True, the Matterhorn's are more calculable and predictable, but that does not prove unconsciousness. Human action also is predictable to some extent. And the more wise and unified a man is—the nearer he approximates to ideal perfection—the more accurately we can predict his response to a given stimulus. We might almost argue, on these lines, that inorganic matter has a certain superiority; for it is not capricious. It knows what it wants to do, and does it; or at least—if this is going too far—it does things, and does them *as if* it knew very well what it wanted to do. To the same conditions and stimuli it always responds in the same way, like reflex action in living beings, and like association in ordinary consciousness. Water always boils punctually at 100°C., and freezes at 0°C., if the pressure is 760mm. of mercury. "Canal" always makes me

94

think of Panama and Mars—though to other people it might suggest Suez, their different experience having given them other association-couplings. But any one knowing me well, or knowing any one well, could say almost certainly what associations "canal" would have—what thought it will evoke. And the same thing is true, to a less extent, of our actions. If a man hits Jack Johnson, the latter will probably hit back. Still more certain is it that no one will hit him unless drunk or insane or in some sort of very exceptional circumstances. If, on the other hand, somebody hits me, the outcome is less certain. It will depend to a greater extent on the result of reflection and judgment—perhaps partly on my estimate of the other fellow's weight, age, training and science! Yet anyone knowing me well, and perceiving the main conditions, could predict with fair approach to accuracy what I should do. Yet I am undoubtedly a conscious being. Some actions of conscious beings, then, are predictable, if we know the conditions. Indeed, in the mass, human action is calculable with precision— witness the various kinds of insurance. Why then deny consciousness to the Matterhorn, because *all* its actions are calculable and predictable? The difference is one of degree, not kind. And indeed *are* all its actions predictable? The fact is, they are only hypothetically so. We say that they would be if we knew enough. But we might say the same of the actions of a man. The truth is, that if we say it of either we are arguing dangerously, from our ignorance and not from our knowledge. It is indeed as risky to say that we could predict the Matterhorn's actions *in toto*, as to say that we cannot predict the man's; for we are continually finding that matter does things which we did not formerly suspect—*e.g.* radio-activity. Clearly, we cannot predict all the activities of the Matterhorn: many may depend on undiscovered properties. So it seems that even if some human actions, such as Newton's discovery of the law of gravitation and Milton's *Paradise Lost* and Spencer's Synthetic Philosophy and Raphael's Sistine Madonna, are strictly unpredictable, it still does not sufficiently differentiate us from the Matterhorn, which on its part also has its unpredictabilities.

As to what parts of matter have separate spirits—where the Snowdon-spirit ends and the Moel Siabod spirit begins, and so on—we need not trouble much about that. This individualising of parts is a reasonable supposition, but it is not necessary to press it. Mr Maurice Hewlett has seen the *genius loci* of a sunny woodland landscape translated into human idiom as an opulent Titianesque beauty (*Lore of Proserpine*), and Manfred sees or feels a spirit of the Alps; but these are details. The only thing that matters is the ensoulment of the earth as a whole. No doubt its spirit-part is divided up somehow, correspondent to its material conformation, as our spirits are divided from each other. The division, however, is not a hermetic sealing off. The universe is continuous. Indeed its parts are inter-penetrative, for every particle influences every other particle—and a thing cannot act where it is not. Similarly, human beings are found to have modes of communication other than those hitherto recognised by orthodox science, and are somehow able to influence others without regard to distance. We seem to be connected with each other in the unseen, subliminal, spiritual region. Our separateness is illusory. So with individualisations of earth-features. They have individual aspects, both on the physical and spiritual side; but they are part of the one earth and its one spirit, as we ourselves are. And that earth-spirit is part of the universe-spirit or God, as the human spirit is part of the earth-spirit.

It is perhaps difficult, at first, to think of the earth as having a life and consciousness of its own, for we are located at little points, and do not see it whole, nor do we see from the inside. We are like an eye which looks at the body of which it forms a part, and finds it difficult to believe in auditory, tactile, olfactory experience; more difficult still to conceive of pure thought, emotion, will. If the earth seems a dead lump, however, think of the human brain. It is a mere lump of whitish filaments, *seen from outside*. But its inner experience is the rich and infinitely detailed life of a human being. So also may the inner experience of the earth be incomparably richer than its outer appearance

96

indicates to our external senses. Objectively, our brains are part of the earth: subjectively, *we see in ourselves a part of what the earth sees in itself.*

In thinking of the earth as an organised being, we must guard against the error of the ancients who called it an animal. It is not an animal. It is a Being of a higher character than any animal, for it includes all animals and all human beings, comprising in its spirit all their spiritual activities, and having its own activities as well. We are to it, as our blood-corpuscles are to us; and to think of the earth-spirit as being like our spirits would be equivalent to a blood-corpuscle thinking of its containing body as another corpuscle, only bigger. Whereas the truth is that a man has feelings and cognitions and purposes, and performs acts, which the corpuscles cannot in the least comprehend. (Somewhat similarly, a drop cannot have waves, or a small celestial body an atmosphere; the lower cannot have what the higher has, nor can it understand it.) The corpuscle may know or believe that its conscience or intuition is a sort of leakage down to it, of the mind or will of its greater self (the voice of its God), and that in so far as it does its duty according to its lights it is assisting the purposes of that higher Being of which it forms a part; and this faith is its highest wisdom. So with us. Human duty, done sincerely according to our lights, is furthering the purposes of the higher Being in whom we live and move. This faith is our highest wisdom concerning our relation to the earth-spirit. We see, then, that there is a good deal of sense in faith and intuition. They are rationally justified. By them we are dimly in touch with the over-soul on our inner side: not *really* dimly, for the connection is close and real, but dimly to our normal consciousness. The connection *via* intellect is an external, round-about affair, necessary and useful, but different. We need to cultivate both. This is the essence of the philosophy of Bergson. There is more than one way of receiving truth. Science is apt to overlook the intuitional way.

On this conscience-side or moral aspect, the Fechnerian idea is particularly fruitful and illuminating. The analogy of our own mind is once more the key—the mirror wherewith to view the greater landscape, the village wherefrom to draw inferences about nations. In childhood, the world is, as James said, a big, blooming, buzzing confusion: sensations pour in quite unconnected; the baby sees the moon, and stretches out an arm to grab it, thus learning that it is not grabable. It is only gradually that the child learns to associate sounds with sights; to know what sounds indicate its mother's presence or proximity, and what sounds its father's. Gradually, individual experiences get linked up and harmonised. Then other disjointednesses arise. Foolish impulses war against better judgment and parents' advice, and the youth's mind is "torn", as we say, very aptly describing the feeling. Growing older and wiser, his mind becomes more unified and consequently more calm. His powers are marshalled and directed consciously at a goal or goals. Wayward impulses are reined in. We feel that poise and strength and wisdom are attained: never perfectly and ideally, but at least to a considerable degree, as compared with the earlier state.

So with the earth-spirit. Being far greater than the human subsidiary spirits, it is longer in coming to maturity. Its elements are still largely at loggerheads with each other. The nations war against each other, and universal peace seems a long time in coming. But steadily, steadily works the earth-spirit, and the nations almost unconsciously—like somnambulists—carry out its will. They are working, consciously or unconsciously, towards universal at-one-ment. A League of Nations has arisen, and the Federation of the World is in sight. Union is the political watch-word. Labour is combining throughout the world. East is learning from West, and West from East. China sends her students to Oxford, Cambridge, Paris, Harvard, and welcomes Western methods. India repays our civilising with the poems of Tagore. In trade, thousands of small businesses are unified in a few great combines, preparing for some sort of Socialism. Finance spreads

98

its world-wide network. Science is becoming international. The frontiers are melting; coalescence, unity, harmony are being achieved. The earth-spirit is reconciling its warring elements. When it succeeds in the complete reconciliation; when the era of universal peace and brotherhood shall dawn; when it reaches its huge equivalent of the ripe, calm, contented wisdom of human age—ah, then will come a state of things which we can but dimly prefigure. But it will come. The age of gold is in the future, not the past. It is our duty and our privilege to hasten the coming of this millennium. And even this is not the end. We cannot conceive the things that shall be. Eye hath not seen, or ear heard. Enough for us to know the tendency, and to trust ourselves to it, actively co-operating.

Before beginning, and without an end, As space eternal, and as surety sure, Is fixed a Power divine which moves to good, Only its laws endure.
This is its touch upon the blossomed rose, The fashion of its hand shaped lotus-leaves; In dark soil and the silence of the seeds The robe of Spring it weaves.
It maketh and unmaketh, mending all; What it hath wrought is better than had been; Slow grows the splendid pattern that it plans, Its wistful hands between.
This is its work upon the things ye see: The unseen things are more; men's hearts and minds, The thoughts of peoples and their ways and wills, Those, too, the great Law binds. —Sir Edwin Arnold, *Light of Asia*.

Is it asked: "Who is the Law-giver, and to what end is the Law?" The question is foolish. Parts cannot know wholes, and the whole does not want parts to be anything but what they obviously are. Each fits into its place, and can do useful work there. Let it keep to tasks "of a size with its capacity"—as à Kempis says—and leave the rest. "What doth the Lord require of thee but to do justly and to love mercy and to walk humbly with thy God?"

RELIGIOUS BELIEF AFTER THE WAR

There is naturally and rightly a great deal of anxiety in the minds of most thoughtful people as to the state of religion after the war. The old order seems to have come down in chaos about our ears, and we are wondering what shape the new building will take. Even our clergy, or some of them, are honestly confessing that beliefs can never be just the same again; to name only two things, they feel that the literal acceptance of the non-resistance doctrine is no longer unqualifiedly possible, as many were formerly inclined to maintain; for the aggression of Germany has made clear the necessity of resisting evil; second, that the old Protestant doctrine of immediate heaven or hell cannot satisfactorily be applied to many of the millions of young fellows who have gone over; some idea of more gradual progress through an intermediate state seems more reasonable. But will this be sufficient? Shall we jog on again, after this world-shaking cataclysm, with such a very microscopical trimming—such an almost imperceptible sail-reefing—as this? Will not rather the whole theological scheme have to be remodelled? Can nations which have suffered as the belligerents have suffered—even those at home, still more the brave lads who have gone through experiences such as they never dreamed of in their worst nightmares—can these people, even if they wish, accept the old scheme, or anything like it?

I am not going to try to answer such a large question directly. Mr Wells has attempted something of the sort in his book, *God the Invisible King*, and he prophesies a religious revolution. It may come as he thinks, but it is perhaps more probable that, in spite of the most earth-shaking events, a certain continuity of thought will be maintained. New religions are not manufactured complete while you wait, like Pallas emerging full-armed from the head of Zeus; or, if they are, by such brilliant Olympians as Mr Wells, they do not get themselves accepted. But there probably will be enough of a change to be called a very considerable thought-revolution, even allowing for some inevitable continuity; and inasmuch as each expression of opinion counts as a datum and as a directive agency, I venture to make my prophecy. And I avoid the negative side, also any argument as to whether or why this or that particular doctrine will become obsolete; I think it better to let obsolescent beliefs drop quietly into their limbo, and to concern ourselves with the living ones that will replace them.

First and most important, the idea of God. We have heard, over and over again, the pathetic cry: "Why does God permit such things? Surely He must be either not All-good or not Almighty?" And one hears of men, even among the clergy, whose minds have been clouded by this difficulty. Mr Wells solves the problem in the fashion of J. S. Mill and the late William James, by postulating a finite god, a good being who is doing his best but who is struggling with a refractory material. To many people this seems a helpful notion, for it saves God's goodness and gives a pleasurable sense of being co-workers with Him in His effort to improve things. But to many of us it is unsatisfactory. Indeed, if one could say such a thing of the author of *Bealby* and of the most genial of modern philosophers, we might say that the finite-god idea seems impossible to anyone with a sense of humour. Is it not really rather ridiculous of us to decide so solemnly that God is no doubt a good fellow but that He is having a tough time of it in fighting Satan, and that there does not seem to be any certainty of His winning? Perhaps the idea appeals to adventurous spirits like Wells and James because it has an air of being a sporting event, and promises excitement; but, I repeat, is it not a rather ridiculous proposition for us small creatures to make? "Finite" and "Infinite" are words; I am not sure that they have any very clear meaning. As to "infinite" in particular, the idea is only a negative one; we think of something finite, and then say "it is not that". But even of "finite", can we say that it has any useful clear meaning? The pen with which I write this may be said to be finite, for I can give its dimensions, and in many ways can define the limits of its powers. But inasmuch as every particle in it attracts every other particle of matter in the universe, the little pen's finiteness or infinity depends on whether the universe itself is finite or infinite; and that is a bigger question than our small wits can settle. And if it is so with a pen, will it not be more so with greater things?

We measure things against the foot-rule of our own selves. We can imagine something much greater than those selves, both physical and spiritual. But when it comes to conceiving the whole physical universe of which we form an insignificant part, I do not feel that we can know whether it is finite or not. It is too big for our foot-rule. Even when dealing with the distances of the stars, we realise that the billions of miles which we can talk about so glibly do not convey much to our minds. We can think of a distance of a few miles fairly clearly, recalling how long it takes us to walk so far; but greater distances soon become mere figures, not representing anything that we can picture. And when we reach the conception of the whole physical universe, we get quite out of our depth. We do not know whether it is finite or infinite; we know only that it is inconceivably greater than we are.

So with the spirit which energises through it. Beginning with what we know best, we find ourselves acquainted with a world of mental phenomena bound together in and by what we call our self. Whatever we think of Hume's argument that a mass of experiences do not involve a soul that has them, it is reasonable and useful to have a name for the active thing which perceives and thinks and acts and feels, whether we call it soul or spirit or mind or self or x. It is something which maintains a sort of identity, in spite of growth and change; and it is marked off from other selves. John Smith has John Smith's experiences, not William Jones's. This individual spirit energises through each of our bodies. Of our own spirit we have a very close knowledge, of other spirits we have a rather more remote knowledge from inference; we infer their states of mind from the states of body which we observe, or from the material effects which they cause in speaking or writing. Passing from the inferred human spirits (inferred because certain lumps of matter act in a way similar to that of the lumps which we call our own bodies), we come to other and larger and very different pieces of matter such as planets. It may seem at the first glance an absurd idea, but I for one cannot think of matter as dead, or of a whole planet without any soul except what is in the human bodies which make up an infinitesimal portion of its mass. It seems to me that there must be some sort of mind energising through the planet-mass as my own mind energises through my body-mass. And, carrying the idea further, we arrive at a conception of the whole universe as ensouled by a Being who in the material immanent manifestation is the Logos of the Christian doctrine, but who also transcends the material part as indeed the Christian doctrine teaches. This spirit, transcending the physical universe as well as energising through it, is greater in comparison with our spirits than the physical universe is in comparison with our bodies. Therefore, once more, and to a greater degree, we are out of our depth. To throw words like finite and infinite at such a Being is to make ourselves ridiculous. It is like a microbe sticking its own adjective-labels—if it has any—on a man, whom the microbe's vocabulary as a matter of fact will not apply to. God is too great for our measure. He is high as heaven; what canst thou do? deeper than Sheol; what canst thou know? The measure thereof is longer than the earth, and broader than the sea—yea, than the whole universe itself.

This conclusion of Zophar the Naamathite, acquiesced in by Job at the end of the argument, seems to some minds an evaporation of God into an Absolute without any human attributes. We feel the necessity or at least the desirability of regarding Him as good, loving, etc., and we shrink from any de-personalisation. But there is a way out of the difficulty. God is incomprehensible, as the Creed says; parts cannot comprehend wholes. But there is something deep in us, call it what you will, which tells us that our ideals of Good, Truth, and Beauty are divine; are God in so far as we are able to cognise Him. Good, true, beautiful actions and thoughts are God manifested through our personal limitations; they are rainbow colours broken out of the pure white light of God. We do right to worship them. They are the highest we can comprehend, though we may reach lame hands of faith to the apprehension of the Unconditioned. But this is a very great mystery, revealed only to the mystic. And it is a dangerous path, for by reaching "beyond good and evil" we lose touch with humanity and with the virtues we can exercise, risking the insanity to which Nietzsche so logically succumbed. We may dimly apprehend the Incomprehensible, but we must live and work among comprehensibilities. That is what we are here for. God is conceived by us—and rightly so conceived—as Good, Truth, Beauty, though we can see that as He really is He must transcend them. Mr Wells's distinction between the Finite God and the Veiled Being is not an ultimate. The two are one, seen as two because of our limitations. They are the rainbow and its source. The sun cannot be looked upon directly, but only when dimmed or reflected.

Then as to immortality. The deaths of so many of our best, and the sorrow thus brought into almost every home, force this question into prominence. If blank pessimism is to be avoided, many people feel that they must have some assurance of the continued existence of those who have made the supreme sacrifice—a sacrifice at the call of duty, greater probably than any sacrifice ever made by us of the older generation who have lived in the smooth times of peace. We feel that if these magnificent young lives have come to nought, have been *wasted*, there is no rational religious belief possible to us. Accordingly we inquire about immortality. And, curiously enough, Science, which in the last generation tended to deny or discredit individual survival of bodily death, now gives a quite opposite verdict. Psychical research brings forward scientific evidence for that welcome belief. It seems too good to be true; but it is true. Public opinion has not yet fully accepted it—nor is it well that opinion should change too rapidly—for it was well drenched in materialism during the heyday of physical science and its astonishing applications in the latter part of the nineteenth century, but the leaders of thought in almost all branches—scientific, legal, literary, and what not—are now admitting that the evidence is at least surprising, and those who have studied it most are one by one announcing that it is convincing. There are many questions yet to solve, such as the nature and occupations of the future life, concerning which there are different views, and the problems may turn out to be insoluble; but the main problem seems on the way to be settled. The survival of human personality is a fact. And the indications, so far as we have got, suggest that the next stage is a life of opportunity, work, progress, even more than the present one. There is much to be thankful for in even this only incipient revelation. It is salvation great and joyous, to those reared amid unacceptable theories of a blank materialism or the much more dreadful hell-doctrines of the theologians.

The religion of the coming time, then, seems likely to be mainly based on these two articles, belief in God in the way indicated, and belief in survival and progress on the other side. Both beliefs are empirical, and are thus in harmony with the temper of our time. They begin with the things which are most real to us, first the fact of conscious experience, then the external world, and reason upward therefrom, instead of beginning with metaphysical entities and attributes, and reasoning down—and failing to establish contact with the material world. Religious experience there still may be, and this may give rise to quite new and unexpected forms of belief or worship; but on the whole the tendency of thought for the last three hundred years has been increasingly empirical, and the success of the method is likely to ensure its continuance. It may be true that the ideal world is the more real—probably it is—that out of thought's interior sphere these phenomenal wonders of the world rose to upper air, as Emerson says; but for us in the present circumstances the way back to universe-spiritualisation is *via* experience (and mainly sense-presentations) carefully observed and studied. If these scientific methods, which are open to everybody, can lead to belief in God and a spiritual world to which we pass at death, it seems unnecessary to return to the bad old days when sporadic experiences of this or that ecstatic, or logic-chopping by this or that theologian, led to beliefs and cults of widely differing character according to the idiosyncracy of the writer. A method which is open to all and the rules of which are agreed on will be likely to yield something like unanimity. The churches may yet form one fold, if they will; in which, with variations to satisfy different æsthetic or symbolistic needs, all souls may find the answer to their queries, healing for their sorrow, and scope for their reverence and love; in a word, salvation.